Successful Selling

SUCCESSFUL SELLING

A *self-help guide using cognitive-behavioral techniques*

Judy Proudfoot

Robinson
LONDON

Robinson Publishing Ltd
7 Kensington Church Court
London W8 4SP

First published by Robinson Publishing Ltd 1999
Copyright © Judy Proudfoot 1999

A copy of the British Library Cataloguing in Publication Data for this
title is available from the British Library.

ISBN 1-84119-083-7

Printed and bound in the EC

Contents

Foreword

Successful Selling is based on the latest research and experience in the psychology of success. It is designed to assist anyone in selling to achieve more by learning some of the specific patterns of thinking and behaviour that underpin success. The programme contained in this book is skills-based, practical and relevant, and founded on sound cognitive (mental) and behavioral techniques. It follows the main principles and processes of cognitive-behavioral therapy, which has a very fine pedigree stretching back over many decades. I have applied them to the role of selling, and have been able to show through my research over the past eight years, that they significantly improve success in selling.

Objectives

As a result of reading this book and carrying out the tasks and other activities contained in it, you will be able to:

- identify key attitudes and behaviour that enhance your personal effectiveness;
- recognize and evaluate the specific thoughts and beliefs that are guiding your work;
- develop attitudes and behaviour that will lead to increased initiative, resilience and success.

Who is this suitable for?

Successful Selling is ideal for individuals who wish to improve their personal effectiveness and their resistance to the undermining effects of setbacks and rejections. It is especially relevant for those who are experiencing a rough patch, but is valuable for all who are keen to achieve greater success.

How does it work?

This programme contained in *Successful Selling* is based on a very powerful set of cognitive and behavioral strategies. The techniques will be presented in sequence, with each stage building on the previous one. For this reason, **it is necessary to complete all seven stages.** If you skip one, you will not understand the next.

At various places throughout the text, you will be asked to reflect on the usefulness of what you've read, or to undertake exercises to try out the techniques. Some of the exercises may seem detailed and slow, but this is to give you the opportunity to analyse your thinking and behaviour. It's like slowing down a movie in order to look at the frames individually. Once you have absorbed the techniques, you'll be able speed up the movie again.

However, completing the seven stages and their activities is just the start. In fact, only one-third of the benefit comes from what you will learn in the book itself. The remaining two-thirds will be acquired by using the strategies in your work. To help you do this, there are tasks for you to complete at the end of each stage. I suggest that you allow about a week between each of the stages in order to complete the activities.

The behavioral strategies – such as high-performance goal-setting, effective planning and creative time management – are introduced early in the book. These have been specifically customized to the role of selling, and form the basis on which the mental strategies are introduced.

These mental strategies are also introduced sequentially and have also been customized to the role of selling. Each strategy is presented according to a format designed to optimize learning:

- the technique is explained with examples;

- you then try out the technique, using hypothetical selling activities;

- you apply the technique to your own selling issues;

- you practise the technique during the week in your sales work.

To help you gain maximum benefit from the programme, I have included a Personal Log for you to complete. At the end of each stage of the book, you will be asked to note down any insight you have gained or things you have learned about yourself or your job.

The aim is to keep instruction to a minimum, and to present the programme contained in the book as a process of investigation and experimentation. You are encouraged to take a 'scientific' approach to the course content – that is, to try out the techniques for a period of time, discard those that don't work for you and practise those that do, so that less helpful ways of thinking and acting are replaced with high-performance attitudes and behaviour.

Acknowledgements

This programme was developed by Dr Judy Proudfoot who would like to acknowledge all external assistance received, including the ideas incorporated in *Optimism ABC* by Dr M. E. P. Seligman and Foresight Inc.; *The Feeling Good Handbook* by Dr David Burns; *Cognitive Therapy of Depression* by A. T. Beck, A. J. Rush, B. F. Shaw and G. Emery; *Reason and Emotion in Psychotherapy* by A. Ellis; as well as the advice and input from Dr Melanie Marks, Mr Frank Thaxton and Mr Jim McDonald.

Introduction

Selling is a fascinating job. On the one hand, it has many rewards: it is varied, the earnings can be very high, and it often allows considerable freedom in the way the work is carried out. But it can also be a lonely job, characterized by rejections and knock-backs as well as severe sales targets, which can lead to feelings of stress and demoralization. Earning on a commission basis can add to the strain, and it is well known for many people who start out in selling to no longer be in it five years later.

So what is the secret of successful selling? Well, first you need to have specific skills and abilities. For example, you need to know how to generate sales leads, approach potential customers, create interest in your product or service, gain commitment, close the sale. But successful selling requires much more – you also need to have a successful attitude. Success depends as much on your beliefs as on your skills, abilities and experience.

This book is about developing a successful attitude for selling. It is not a 'how to' in selling skills – there are many other good books about that. This one will show you ways to enhance your success in selling by managing the way you *think*.

Our beliefs about ourselves, our work and other people are the glasses through which we view the world. They are the 'rules' we've developed over the years to guide our daily actions. For example, some people have a strong belief that, if they commit themselves to do something, they must deliver. Other common beliefs are: 'If I do not prepare, I will be less effective'; 'People should be treated with fairness and honesty'; 'I must do well at everything I undertake.' Our beliefs organize our thinking and govern our behaviour – and they determine how successful we are.

Beliefs about *why* events occur are of particular importance in selling. Each of us has a habitual way of explaining good and bad events; this is our 'attributional style'. There is strong research evidence that a salesperson's attributional style affects both the quantity and quality of sales that he or she makes. For example, salespeople who tend to attribute their individual successes to external, temporary factors – such as 'I had a lucky break with that client' – will be less successful overall than their colleagues who make a point of looking for the part they themselves have played in positive outcomes, particularly if it's something they can do again in different situations.

Our beliefs create self-fulfilling prophesies. They can lead us to block out some relevant facts and focus too greatly on others. They can therefore limit our creativity, reduce our flexibility and undermine our success. For example, if you believe that you're weak in selling certain products or services, you won't see opportunities to sell them effectively. You'll be convinced that you just can't do it. On the other hand, our beliefs can also work to our advantage, helping us to focus our attention, process information efficiently, react to situations quickly.

Have you ever asked yourself what beliefs have you developed about yourself and others over the years? How do they affect what you do? Are they enhancing your success or are they holding you back?

This book will help you to become aware of the specific beliefs that are guiding your thinking and actions. It will also assist you in ascertaining whether they're helpful or not, and if they're holding you back, it will show you how to develop new ways of thinking.

Successful selling takes ambition and drive; it also demands psychological resilience to withstand the inevitable rejections and setbacks. It's about creating 'opportunity thinking' – looking for possibilities, solutions, new ways of tackling situations – rather than 'obstacle thinking': focusing on difficulties, problems and reasons for giving up.

When you change the way you think, your feelings and behaviour change. And when you feel and behave differently, you get different results. This is the 'cognitive' part of the 'cognitive-behavioral method' – changing the way you think. Of course, it's also possible to increase your personal effectiveness by working directly on your behaviour and learning new skills and ways of doing things. This book will also teach you some types of behaviour associated with success in selling, such as setting high-performance goals, planning your work effectively and managing your time creatively. But the primary focus will be on helping you to manage your thinking – your attitudes, expectations and beliefs – in order to become more successful.

Success can be compared with the star ratings given to hotels – it is on a continuum. Some people are three-star hotels, others are the equivalent of five-star hotels and, as someone who tried out these techniques said jokingly, 'still others are "bed & breakfasts".'

How would you classify yourself?

No matter at what stage of success you are currently, this programme will help you up to the next one.

So, let's get started.

Stage 1:

The ABC of Success

We all know that success breeds success. One success leads to another and another and so on. But does this mean that we have to wait until a success happens along in order to become more successful? Is this the only way to success? The answer, of course, is no. There is a more direct path – through your thinking and actions.

Let's start with the first key attitude for success – motivation. Successful selling requires *sustained motivation in the face of rejections, difficulties and setbacks*.

But do you know what motivates you?

On a piece of paper, draw up two lists: the types of things that motivate you and those that *de*motivate you.

Motivation is affected by two different groups of factors. On the one hand, it's affected by factors *external* to us, such as the situation in which we find ourselves, our interactions with others and so on. On the other hand, our motivation and performance are affected in a large way by *internal* factors, such as our behaviour and our thoughts – that is, the interpretations we make of our experiences.

Refer back to your list and label your motivators and demotivators as either 'E' for external or 'I' for internal. Sometimes we have no control over the external factors that can motivate or demotivate us. What we can control, and indeed change, are our behaviour and interpretation of events.

Motivation, and indeed success in general, are related to:

- the activities we engage in (our behaviour);
- the way we interpret our experiences (our thoughts or 'self-talk').

Activities associated with success

Some activities enhance motivation and drive – for example, identifying good sales leads, using state-of-the-art sales tools and techniques, closing a sale, achieving a target, completing a difficult task, engaging in a sport or exercise.

Other activities are associated with displeasure, producing negative moods, such as disillusionment, demotivation, stress and so on. Examples include dealing with unpleasant clients, juggling too many tasks, working with unreasonable targets, selling poor products, having inadequate support, receiving unconstructive criticism.

Research has shown that our mood on any one day is related to the number of positive and negative activities we engage in during that day. Thus what we do – or don't do – can have a profound influence on how we feel and perform in selling.

But are you aware of what *specific activities* result in you feeling more or less motivated, energetic and personally effective? Are you in control of your motivation or are you at the mercy of external factors?

Task

During the next week, take note of the activities you engage in to see what effect they have on your motivation.

There's a form provided at the end of this chapter to help you do this. For each activity, rate on a scale of 0 to 5 the degree of achievement and pleasure you get from it. For example, you might rate a workout at the gym 3 out of 5 for achievement and 5 out of 5 for pleasure. At the end of each day, rate your overall motivation for the day.

In Stage 2, I'll help you to develop a list of your 'Personal Motivating Activities', those that will help you to maintain your energy and drive. We'll work on other activities associated with success in the next stage, too.

Thinking associated with success

The second major influence on your motivation and personal effectiveness is the way you *think*. If you think negative thoughts about your job – for example, 'These sales leads are useless' – or pessimistic thoughts about the future – for instance, 'We're heading for a recession and people just won't buy' – you're bound to feel demotivated. On the other hand, if you think, 'This is a temporary setback. I may as well try to get something out of it,' you're unlikely to feel so down.

The first point to learn about the ABC of success is that the same situation can be interpreted in a number of different ways, leading to vastly different outcomes.

How thoughts influence feelings

I'd like you to undertake a short exercise to illustrate how your thoughts affect how you feel. Take a piece of paper and divide it into two columns. At the head of the first column, write the word 'THOUGHTS' and at the head of the second, write 'FEELINGS/ACTIONS'. Now read the following scenario slowly and try to imagine it vividly.

Imagine you have arranged to meet a friend in a restaurant. You haven't been to that restaurant before, and it's quite a distance from where you work. You leave the office in plenty of time and get there about five minutes early. You walk in. The restaurant is not too full, but as you wait, two groups of people come in. You think to yourself, 'I'll wait for my friend before I order.' You reflect on your day's activities. You look at your watch. The restaurant is starting to fill up. Others who had been there alone have now been joined by friends. You begin to wonder what has happened to yours. You order a drink and take a few sips. You look at your watch again. Your friend is quite late now. Most of the other people in the restaurant are having a good time. There are not many on their own … like you.

You should now try to 'capture' your thoughts and then, separately, your feelings about this situation.

In the first column on your piece of paper, jot down words or phrases that represent what was going through your mind as you were imagining the restaurant scene. In the second column, write down words or phrases that represent your feelings or actions.

Now, as an experiment, ask some family members, friends or work colleagues to carry out the same exercise. Compare what they have written in the two columns with what you did.

Here's what some people who carried out this activity wrote down. 'I've bothered to get here on time – why hasn't she?' (*feeling*: irritated). 'I hope he hasn't had an accident' (*feeling*: worried). 'Everyone will think: "What's the matter with her sitting there all on her own?"' (*feeling*: embarrassment). 'I've been stood up!' (*feeling*: upset). 'Maybe I've got the time or place wrong' (*feeling*: concerned).

People react differently to the same event based on what they say to themselves about it and how they interpret it. In the restaurant scenario, for instance, the situation was the same for you and the other people, but since each of you put your own interpretations on it, completely different reactions are the likely result.

Many people believe that feelings – such as motivation, confidence and satisfaction on the one hand, and stress, worry and frustration on the other – all result from factors beyond their control. These can include policies of the company they work for, the state of the economy, family matters, a childhood event, their body chemistry, their health. Certainly some of our feelings are caused by external factors. But much of what we feel and do is the result of the way we *interpret* a situation rather than the situation itself. It is our thoughts and attitudes that primarily create our feelings and behaviour, and these can , in turn, affect our performance.

We can't control external events, but we can learn to control our thinking in order to become more confident, motivated, enterprising and successful. The key to this is the ABC model.

The ABC model

A   stands for the *antecedent* – that is, some action, event or situation.

B   stands for your *belief* – that is, your thoughts about or interpretation of the action or event.

C   stands for the *consequences* – your resulting feelings and behaviour ... and performance.

The ABC model

> ### Antecedent
> Action, event, situation

> ### Belief
> Thoughts, interpretations

> ### Consequences
> Feelings, behaviour, performance

There is a close relationship between thoughts, feelings and behaviour. The first two of this trio are sometimes confused. A *feeling* is an emotional state – for example, satisfaction, confidence, doubt, worry. A *thought* is an idea or a notion. People often wrongly use phrases such as 'I feel like …' or 'I felt …' to express thoughts. For instance, they say, 'I felt that I'd gone as far as I could' or 'I feel out of place.' However, they really don't mean that they have a 'feeling'; instead they are expressing a strongly held thought.

Complete the ABCs

See if you can differentiate between thoughts and feelings by filling in the chart below.* Imagine each of the situations, as well as the thought or feeling provided. Then fill in the blanks, making sure that the thoughts match the feelings and actions. The first example has been completed for you.

* Adapted from *Learned Optimism* by Dr M. E. P. Seligman.

Antecedent/event	Beliefs/thoughts	Consequences/feelings and/or actions
1 You are held up in traffic	I'm going to miss my appointment	Stressed
2 You are learning an important new technique, and others catch on more quickly than you		Depressed
3 You are learning an important new technique, and others catch on more quickly than you		Relaxed
4 Your manager passes you in the corridor and doesn't acknowledge you	What's the matter with him/her today?	
5 Your manager passes you in the corridor and doesn't acknowledge you	I must have done something to upset him/her	
6 You've received a complaint from a customer		Irritated
7 You've received a complaint from a customer		Concerned
8 You are waiting for a phone call that doesn't come	How inconsiderate. I've wasted a whole afternoon waiting for this call	

Can you see from this exercise how a person's thoughts strongly affect how they feel and behave?

Here are some possible answers to each of the examples. Are they similar to yours?

Antecedent 2/*Thought*: 'I'm stupid.'

Antecedent 3/*Thought*: 'That's OK. They've had a head start. I'll catch up.'

Antecedent 4/*Feeling*: Curious. *Action*: Ask others if they know.

Antecedent 5/*Feeling*: Concern. *Action*: Do a mental action-replay of recent interactions with him/her.

Antecedent 6/*Thought*: 'Some customers complain about everything.'

Antecedent 7/*Thought*: 'Maybe I've done something wrong.'

Antecedent 8/*Feeling*: Annoyed.

The point of the 'Complete the ABCs' exercise is to demonstrate how our feelings and behaviour are influenced by what we think. This is particularly true in selling. Most of our thinking is accurate and helpful, producing appropriate feelings and behaviour. For example, if you have suffered a setback, it is natural to feel disappointed. But some ways of thinking can be exaggerated and unhelpful, which leaves you feeling pessimistic or fed up, which, in turn, affects your selling.

However, you do not need to be a victim of your thinking. With effort and practice, you can change your thinking style and, as a result, experience more motivation and success.

This does not mean fooling yourself or being unrealistic. It means learning to check whether your thoughts are accurate and, if not, changing them to more helpful views.

Four steps to success

- Recognize your thoughts.
- Determine whether your thoughts lead to helpful feelings and behaviour.
- If these are unhelpful, substitute more effective ways of thinking.
- Practise new ways of thinking until they become habits.

Let's look at two examples of how thoughts can affect feelings, and how a change in perspective can cause a change in feelings, behaviour ... and results.

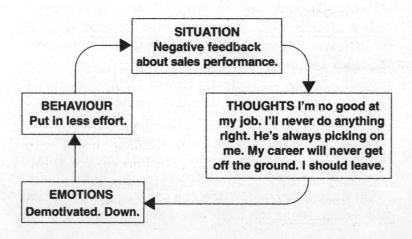

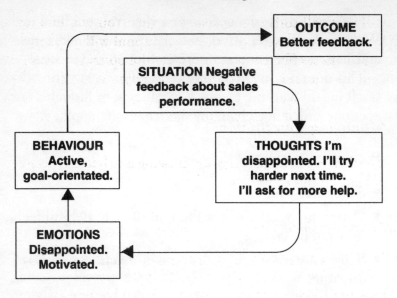

Motivation, confidence and resilience are related both to the *activities* you engage in and to your *thoughts* or *attitudes*. Studies have shown that the best way to enhance success is not to try to change these feelings directly (say, via a motivation 'pill'), but to change your thoughts and attitudes as well as the activities you engage in. A change in feelings will follow – you will become more confident, more motivated, more resilient to setbacks and more optimistic. A feedback loop then occurs. The feelings affect your activities and thoughts, which make you even more effective and so it goes on.

On the reverse side, when you're feeling demoralized and fed up, you're less likely to want to do things and you will think all sorts of negative thoughts. You will end up feeling even worse, and a downward spiral will develop.

The most effective way to reverse this spiral is to intervene in two areas – your thinking and your actions.

Managing your thinking

The first step in managing your thinking is to become aware of your thoughts.

Automatic thoughts

Each of us carries on a constant internal dialogue or 'self-talk' – words or images that flow through our minds. You may not be aware of your self-talk, but it happens all the time and is very normal. For example, as you read this, you may be thinking about something else at the same time.

Automatic thoughts are different from our conscious deliberate thoughts. They are called 'automatic' because they require no effort to produce; they just pop into your head. In addition, they:

- are often in a shorthand/abbreviated form;
- seem plausible;
- can be difficult to turn off.

Some kinds of automatic thoughts lead to success, while others lead to problems and difficulties. For example, if you think 'I'm out of my depth here' when you're making a sales presentation to a tricky client, it will affect how you carry out the presentation.

Self-talk can overpower and control your surface words or behaviour, despite the best of your intentions and sometimes in very unhelpful ways.

Since self-talk is so powerful, it's important to be aware of it, so that you can use it to enhance your success. Obviously the first step towards controlling your thoughts – that is, self-talk – is to catch them!

Thought catching

Noticing what is going through your mind may not come easily. Maybe you're so busy that you're operating on 'automatic pilot' – a salesperson once said to me, 'I don't think, I just *do.*' But we all have automatic thoughts. They flow through our minds all the time, affecting our mood and behaviour. If you're not aware of yours, they could be undermining your personal effectiveness and quality of life.

One clue to catching your thoughts is to notice when there's a shift in your feelings or mood. You can then look back to what was running through your mind immediately beforehand.

Another way of becoming aware of your self-talk and its effect on your sales performance is to learn to record your thoughts. This allows you to stand back and simply observe them as they occur – rather like standing at the side of the road doing a traffic count, instead of standing in the middle of the road getting run over by every car that passes.

It is simply a case of recognizing the thoughts as they occur, jotting them down and, at the end of each day, tallying up the different types of thoughts you have had.

Why don't you try this during the next week? To prepare for it, first gather together a list of common thoughts in selling, using the form below. To get you going, I've provided you with some examples.

Common positive and negative thoughts in selling

POSITIVE THOUGHTS (optimistic, motivating)	NEGATIVE THOUGHTS (pessimistic, demotivating)
I'm well prepared.	Not another time-waster!
This product/service is easy to sell.	I'm never going to be able to close this sale.
I explained that well.	I can't be bothered.
These customers are pleasant.	This is leading nowhere.
Yes!	I'm out of my depth

Once you become aware of your automatic thoughts, the next step is to evaluate them to see if they are enhancing your success or holding you back. I'll show you how to do this in Stage 3. But first I want us to look at some of the key actions and behaviour that build success in selling. This is what we'll do in Stage 2.

Next week's tasks

1 Monitor your activities for a week to see when you feel most optimistic and motivated and which activities are associated with these feelings.

On the Diary of motivation, note all of your **activities** during the week. (Remember: trivial activities are just as important as major ones.) For each activity you engage in, rate (on the form below) the amount of **achievement** you feel (0=no achievement, 5=a great deal of achievement) and the **pleasure** you get from it (0=no pleasure, 5=a great deal of pleasure) – for example, 'Gym workout A4 P5.'

Then, at the end of each day, give an overall rating (0–5) for your **motivation** for the day.

2 'Catch' your automatic thoughts on a daily basis for a week and note the actual thoughts on the form on page 17 (blank copies are provided in the Appendix). To assist yourself, use the list of thoughts that you have already compiled on page 13.

At the end of every day, tally up and see how many positive and negative thoughts you have had.

You will probably find that the more positive thoughts and the fewer negative thoughts you have had in a day, the better you feel – that is, more confident, optimistic, motivated and so on. Do not worry if at this stage you seem to be having more negative thoughts. It is just that negative thoughts are easier to notice! The balance will improve as you become better at 'catching' the positive ones.

3 Complete the first week's entry in your Personal Log (page 161): 'Something I have learned (about myself, my job, etc.) which I will find useful.'

Diary of motivation

	......day	......day	......day	......day	......day	......day	......day
Morning							
Afternoon							
Evening							
Overall motivation for the day (0–5)							

 The ABC of Success

Catching thoughts

Date	Positive thoughts	Tally	Negative thoughts	Tally

17

Stage 2:

Actions towards Selling Success

Top sales performers behave in certain key ways as a matter of routine. These actions are noticeably absent from the routines of less successful salespeople, who furthermore often discount their value. Yet the proof is there. There are a number of activities that have been shown to be associated with success in selling. Listed below is a selection of the more important ones.

High-performance goal-setting

Successful salespeople set goals for themselves. They take charge and appoint themselves captains of their own ships instead of bobbing about like corks in the ocean, following any wave that comes along. Having goals gives you a destination to aim for; they help you to set a course to take you where you really want to go.

When I talk about 'goals', I'm not talking about the resolutions that we make each new year and then inevitably forget. There's an art to setting high-performance goals that makes them different from normal goals and objectives. When you set high-performance goals, you start with a dream or vision and work backwards from there.

What is your dream? Ask yourself: if the world was your oyster, what would you want? If you had a magic wand, what would you do? Spend a few minutes now daydreaming. Create a clear, vivid, mental picture of your dream. Resist thinking about *how* you're going to reach it – that will come later. For now, just focus on your dream.

Now write your dream in the box below.

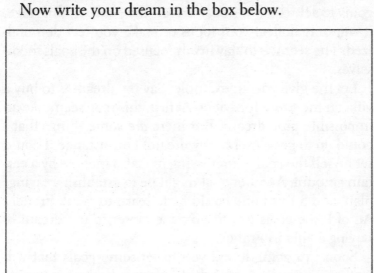

The next step is to convert your dream into goals. High-performance goals have a number of specific advantages. They:

- focus your attention;

- direct your actions;

- keep you on course;

- increase your persistence;

- open your eyes to opportunities.

So how do you set goals that will move you towards your dream?

You do it by working backwards from your dream, making a note of all the things you could do that would lead towards it. At the same time, you need to make sure that you don't allow yourself to slip into considering *how* you're going to achieve – or not achieve – the goals. At this stage, it will only deflect your focus or make you feel demoralized. The secret is to stay firmly focused on the goals themselves.

Let me give you an example. Say my dream is to buy a villa on the French Riviera. At first, this may seem like an impossible pipe dream. But there *are* some things that I could do to get closer to my dream. For instance, I could set myself the goal of increasing my sales income by a certain amount. Another goal might be to establish a savings plan, and a third one could be to learn to speak French. All of these goals would take me closer to my dream of buying a villa in France.

Soon I'm going to ask you to set some goals that will lead to your own dream. But before I do, I want to give you some tips. High-performance goals have a number of distinguishing characteristics.

First, they are phrased **positively**. You say what you want to do or achieve, rather than what you want to stop doing or what you want to change. So, rather than saying, 'I want to reduce my spending', a better goal would be: 'I want to save X amount per year'. Positive goals enable you to step out of current reality and visualize what you want to achieve.

At the same time, goals must be **attainable**. It's no use setting your sights on being an astronaut if you haven't even got a driving licence! High-performance goals should be challenging, but they should not be so difficult that you become demoralized and give up, and not so easy that you don't feel any satisfaction from achieving them.

Your goals also need to be **specific**. Avoid vague goals such as 'I want to be a better salesperson.' It is difficult to know when you have achieved such a goal, because any improvement can be classed as 'better'. Instead, define your goal in specific, measurable terms. Ask yourself what particularly will change when you become a better salesperson. How will you know? You must specify the behaviour or actions that will have to change; don't allow yourself to say, 'I'll just know.' And, more importantly, how will others know? For instance, a specific, measurable goal would be: 'I want to achieve a better balance of sales across the product range by increasing my sales of reproduction furniture to ten items a month.'

So these are the characteristics of high-performance goals. Now it's time to set yours.

In the box below, write down three goals that will lead to your dream.

```
┌────────────────────────────────────────┐
│                                        │
│                                        │
│  1                                     │
│                                        │
│                                        │
│  2                                     │
│                                        │
│                                        │
│  3                                     │
│                                        │
│                                        │
└────────────────────────────────────────┘
```

Now, check your goals.

- Are they each phrased positively?
- Are they attainable?
- Are they specific and measurable?

Having set your goals, now it's time to work out *how* you're going to achieve them. The following technique* may help.

Imagine you are a juggler keeping a number of plates in the air. The plates represent the various aspects of your job, such as selling, customer service, administration, prospecting, accounting and so on. The plates in the air are the aspects of your job with which you are currently involved. Those on the ground are the ones that you are not involved with. You may like to pick up some of the latter; others are there because you have made a conscious decision to not be involved with them for now (or permanently).

Label the plates according to the different aspects of your job. Add extra plates and modify the size of some of the plates if you wish, to reflect their importance or lack of it.

Now ask yourself the following questions. In order to achieve your goals:

Are there any plates that you want to reduce in size or drop altogether? If so, which ones?

....

....

* Adapted from 'Learn to Unwind for Health, Energy, Performance and Wellbeing', NSW Health Department, Australia, 1984.

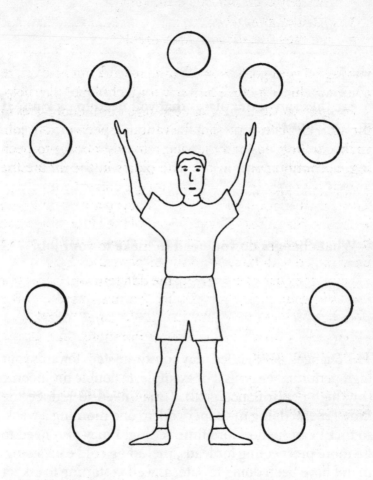

Are there any plates that need to be increased in size? If so, which ones?

....
....

Are there any extra plates that you need to pick up? If so, which ones?

....
....

What changes do you need to make to your job?

....
....

The changes you've listed may constitute steps towards your high-performance goals. For example, to double my income (my high-performance goal), I may need to reduce the time I spend doing my paperwork to one morning a week, so that I can spend more time selling. I may also need to do more prospecting for leads, including cold canvassing, than I have been doing to date, as well as starting to ask for recommendations after each sale I make. These become my sub-goals.

Chose one of the high-performance goals you wrote down on page 21. In the box below, write the sub-goals needed to achieve that goal.

Sub-goals:

1

2

3

Now, for each sub-goal, think about any obstacles or setbacks you might encounter. Then brainstorm ways to overcome them. Be as creative as you can.

Sub-goal 1:

Possible obstacles:

Ways to overcome the obstacles:

Sub-goal 2:

Possible obstacles:

Ways to overcome the obstacles:

Sub-goal 3:

Possible obstacles:

Ways to overcome the obstacles:

Next, you need to devise a way of keeping track of your progress. It is well known that feedback is necessary for goal-setting to improve performance – can you imagine trying to lose weight without ever getting on a set of scales or feeling how loose your clothes have become? You need to build a progress-tracking system into your goals. For example, set up a simple chart to monitor how you get on each week.

Take another look at the sub-goals you've set. What feedback mechanisms can you add to measure your progress? Write them down below.

_____

_____

Your task this week is to make a start on one of your sub-goals. Don't forget to reward yourself when you reach milestones along the way. Some people don't believe in the notion of rewarding themselves, stating that, for them, achieving the milestone is reward enough. But self-rewards are important in the psychology of selling (*see later*). They increase the likelihood of further successes. Try rewarding yourself even if you are sceptical!

Personal motivating activities

Successful salespeople don't rely on external circumstances – such as company awards or managers' feedback – to motivate them. They take responsibility for their own motivation. But, for them, this entails being aware of their personal motivating activities.

Examine your 'Diary of motivation', which you should have completed over the past week. Mark the days on which you felt more optimistic and motivated and then answer the following questions:

- **What activities were you carrying out on those days?**

  _____

  _____

  _____

  _____

- **Did these activities produce ratings of high achievement or high pleasure or both?**

  _____

  _____

- **Is there a link between the type of activities you engaged in, the amount of achievement and pleasure you got from them and how motivated you felt?**

  _____

  _____

- **If so, what was it?**

  _____

  _____

  _____

- **Would these activities generally cause you to feel more motivated and optimistic?**

_____

_____

_____

_____

Now in the box overleaf, jot down the **personal motivating activities** that you have identified through your 'Diary of motivation' (and any additional possibilities you can think of). Your personal motivating activities make you feel invigorated, confident and optimistic.

Make sure that you have a wide variety of these activities so that you can carry out one every day. Here are some that other salespeople have suggested:

- learning new information;
- solving a challenging problem;
- doing something creative;
- listening to music;
- taking a walk;
- adding to my store of collectibles;
- reading;
- treating myself to a luxury.

Try out new activities in order to extend your list.

Personal motivating activities

Activities that have a motivating effect on my mood

....

....

....

....

....

....

....

....

....

....

....

....

....

....

What insights have you gained about yourself from this work on motivation? For example:

- the types of activities that have the greatest effect on your optimism and motivation;

- the areas of your life in which the frequency of motivating activities is high or low.

Write your insights into your Personal Log: Week 2.

Managing time creatively

A third psychological strategy that enhances success in selling is managing time creatively. Many salespeople think that, because they are busy, they are working productively. However, even though they may seem to be a hive of activity, they can be working quite inefficiently, with the possible result that they become tired and turn in a suboptimal performance.

A case history: David

My biggest disappointment was the interview I had after my first three months with the company. I had thought that I had been 100 per cent effective and was going along OK. Then I had the interview with my area manager – it really tore me apart. He picked up on things I hadn't realized that I wasn't doing properly, and he really made me look at myself. I was completely deflated. I decided that I had two choices: either get out of the company or stick at it and prove the manager wrong ... so I stuck at it and proved him wrong!

I took a hard look at myself – and self-criticism is one of the most difficult things you can do. I knew in the back of my mind that, in the months leading up to this, I had been chasing around quite a bit – going back on calls, going to certain areas where I'd been before. I really had to look at what I'd been doing with my time. I asked myself the question: 'What are you doing this week?' And I found that I couldn't answer it.

I sat down with my sales manager and we put together a weekly time management sheet, which has proved to be a great success with me. Poor time management had been the

*major element in my 'downfall'. With that finally put right,
I knew exactly what I was doing in every aspect of the job,
be it customer service, selling, preparation, planning. Without time management, you can forget trying to do the job.*

*Prior to the interview, I was probably putting in 200 per
cent effort but getting nothing out of it. Now I work 'smarter,
not harder'. For the first couple of months, it was a real
effort to use the time management sheets, but after that, I
didn't even notice I was doing it. Now I have a lot more time
for myself. I know exactly what I'm doing and where I'm
going each week, and I'm planning from one week to the
next. It's a much happier way to work.*

*As far as selling is concerned, it's now much more relaxed. I
don't have the pressure of all the admin and correspondence piling up like I did before. I used to put selling and
admin on the same level. Now I stay in the office on Mondays
and clear all my admin, and that's it for another week. The
rest of the week I can devote all my time and put all my
thoughts into selling. I try to achieve 30 calls, ten presentations and three sales a week, and with time management, I
have the time to do that with no problem.*

Gaining control of time

Gaining control of your time and the tasks you need to
complete will have a powerful effect on your motivation
and success.

The first step is to **plan your time**. This will give you
control over the things you need to do. Planning is especially
important when there are other things happening in your
job or in the rest of your life that are not within your control.

There's a weekly plan for you to use at the end of this chapter. First of all, fill in some of the routine things that you'll be doing during the coming week, such as prospecting for clients or doing your correspondence.

Then make a list of all the tasks you need to do next week and rate them in order of importance: 1=the most important, 2=the next most important, 3=the least important. Spread your most important tasks evenly across your plan. Alternatively, you might find that first dealing successfully with one or two minor tasks will start a winning streak that will make working on the bigger ones much easier. Try out different approaches in your plan and find the way that works best for you. The point is to plan important tasks into your week, so that they don't build up to a stress-producing urgency.

The third step is to build some flexible time into your plan – that is, periods during which you haven't allocated any tasks. I normally recommend that two timeslots per week are kept free for this purpose, so that if something unexpected comes up, your plan does not become unworkable. You simply use the flexible slots to accommodate the overrun. And, of course, if nothing unexpected occurs, you can use the flexible-time slots for additional motivating activities or rewards!

The fourth step is to 'carve chunks off the elephant' – that is, **break down large tasks into manageable proportions.** Don't try to eat a whole elephant in one go; you'll get indigestion! Similarly, if you're feeling overwhelmed by jobs that have built up, tackle small chunks at a time. This is the essence of the 'task breakdown technique' *(see below)*.

And, lastly, take a look at your whole plan for the week. Are there any tasks that you can delegate? Have you interspersed boring tasks with jobs that you enjoy? Can you 'multi-task' some of the jobs you need to do, i.e., can you do a couple at the same time? What rewards or pleasant activities have you built into your week?

Task breakdown technique

The hardest part of any job, particularly a boring or overwhelming task, is getting started. For example, take pushing a stalled car: once the wheels turn just a centimetre or so, momentum is on your side and the next centimetre is easier and the next even easier and so on. So it is that, once you have got started on a task, it is much easier to continue than it was to begin in the first place.

If you're feeling overwhelmed by jobs that have been mounting up, the task breakdown technique will help. It consists of breaking a large job down into small manageable steps to help you get started. You don't tackle the whole job – that's what puts you off. Limit yourself to completing just the first step. Once this has been accomplished, the other steps become much easier. Think of the increasing sense of mastery you will feel as you cross off each step!

Below is an example of the task breakdown technique.

Task: Sorting out my tax

1 Phone my tax adviser and make an appointment.

2 Gather together all my bills, receipts and paperwork.

3 Visit the tax adviser and find out what I need to do.

4 Calculate the amount of tax that I owe.

5 Draw up a plan for dealing with future income, expenditure and tax.

6 Write to the tax office with a proposal for paying off the outstanding tax in instalments.

7 Start to pay off the tax according to my plan.

Now try the technique yourself, using the box below. First, make a note of some difficult, unpleasant or boring tasks that you have been avoiding; these can be either work- or home-related. Some work examples might include updating your prospect list, or cold-calling for appointments. Put an asterisk next to the ones to which you could apply the task breakdown technique.

TASKS I HAVE BEEN PUTTING OFF

1

2

3

4

5

Now select one of the tasks that you have asterisked. Break it down into a series of small steps. For each step, give yourself a reward – something pleasurable that you can do when you've completed the step (e.g. a snack, a brief walk).

Task...

Steps	Rewards
1	1
2	2
3	3
4	4
5	5

And, finally, start on the first step. Don't forget to reward yourself when you've completed it.

Rewarding yourself

In the last exercise, you were asked to reward yourself when you completed a step of a particular task. How did you feel about rewarding yourself? What impact did the reward have on your mood?

Asking you to reward yourself is not as childish as it might seem. Years of research in psychology has shown that behaviour is strongly influenced by rewards and punishments. If you want to increase or reinforce a certain type of behaviour, you reward it, and if you want to eliminate it, you either cease rewarding it or you punish it. We also know now that rewards are more effective than punishments or admonitions in bringing about behaviour change, especially in producing long-term changes. These principles are the same whether you are training a pet, teaching a child, influencing another adult or changing your own behaviour.

As adults, we are usually very good at admonishing ourselves, putting ourselves down or concentrating on the one small thing that we did wrong instead of focusing on and rewarding ourselves for the multitude of things we have done well. This is unhelpful. The psychology of success points to a reorientation. Self-rewards are a way to enhance success.

However, to be effective, rewards need to be earned – that is, they must *follow* the desired behaviour. This is known as 'Grandma's Law': 'Eat up your peas, then you can have a treat.' Rewards have a powerful effect on mood as well as behaviour. They help us to focus on our strengths, they reinforce desired behaviour and they improve positive moods. They can be either tangible (e.g. a bar of chocolate) or verbal (e.g. telling yourself: 'Well done!'). Try it this week as an experiment. Think how much better a glass of wine or a beer will taste if you have earned it!

Conclusion

These, then, are the *actions* that are associated with success in selling:

- setting high-performance goals;
- carrying out personal motivating activities;
- managing time creatively;
- rewarding yourself for things well done.

Are they part of your routine?

Next week's tasks

1 Choose one of the sub-goals that you wrote down on page 25. In the box opposite, break this sub-goal into a number of small specific steps. Complete the first step this week, and reward yourself when you have done so. If it is not possible to complete the first step this week, try to break it into even smaller sub-steps and complete the first of those. Then continue, week by week, until all the steps are completed.

Sub-goal ....

Steps	**Rewards**
1	1
2	2
3	3
4	4
5	5

2 Using the Weekly Plan and weekly Prospecting Register (*overleaf*), outline your plan of activity for next week. Make sure that there is a good balance of activities, including some of your own personal motivating activities. In the Prospecting Register, include at least five prospecting approaches to potential clients. You will need these for an exercise later in this book.

Additional blank copies are provided in the Appendix.

Weekly Plan

Week beginning ..../......./.......

	......day	......day	......day	......day	......day	......day	......day
AM							
PM							
Evening							

Prospecting Register

Client/ Prospect	Current Business	Canvass Details	Outcome	Cause of the Outcome

3 Carry out at least one of the personal motivating activities that you listed on page 30. The aim is to confirm its impact on your mood.

4 Complete the second week's entry in your Personal Log: 'Something I have learned (about myself, my job, etc.) which I will find useful.'

Stage 3:

Tuning into Your Thoughts

In Stage 2, we focused on actions that enhance success in selling, such as personal motivating activities, high-performance goal-setting and managing time creatively. But actions are only as good as the thinking behind them.

In this stage, I'm going to show you some techniques that will help you to become more aware of your thinking, so that you can hone it to enhance your success.

Have you ever heard this adage?

> I am able to control only that which I am aware of. That which I am unaware of controls me.

So it is with our thinking. If we are aware of our thoughts, we can take steps to control them. If we're not, they control us.

A case history: Mary

Everybody goes through bad patches. I remember once when I thought that promotion was on the horizon. The company had a vacancy for a sales manager and I thought I was in line for it. But then I found out that they had given it to one of my colleagues instead. That took me back a step or two. I felt rejected and asked myself, 'Why am I doing all this work and then not getting any rewards out of the job?' It obviously crossed my mind whether I might be better rewarded in another company.

I think most people would have these kinds of thoughts when this sort of thing happens. But after a while, you sit back and analyse the situation and then say to yourself, 'Come on, let's start proving some people wrong and let them know where you should be.'

When you get rejected like this, you have negative thoughts at least for a time. Some people can get over them quite quickly, while others take much longer.

It is natural for us all to think and feel negatively when bad events befall us. But instead of being controlled and overwhelmed by these thoughts you can learn to gain control of them, to make them work *for* you rather than *against* you. And one way of doing this is to teach yourself to keep a Thought Record.

Thought records

You will recall that, in Stage 1, we talked about the ABC model. Using this, we could see how, although the situation we're in affects how we feel and act, the *main* influence on our feelings and behaviour is how we interpret the situation – in other words, our thoughts. During that week, you practised 'catching' your automatic thoughts. Did you find that some of them popped up a number of times? Were any of them in shorthand form? Could you see the link between your thoughts and your feelings or behaviour?

The next step in honing your thoughts to enhance your success is to record your thoughts on a Thought Record. Here you describe the situation, your thoughts about it (write down as many as you can), and the feelings or behaviour that resulted. Remember to make your thoughts match your feelings and behaviour. In addition, you should rate how much you believe each thought, on a scale 0–10, and also how strong each of your feelings is (0–10).

Here is an example of a Thought Record.

Thought Record

Situation	Thoughts (Rate how much you believe each thought; scale 0–10)	Feelings (Rate strength 0–10)
Manager has suggested that I increase my personal production	I can't do that amount of business (9) Why me? (5) I'm already working at full capacity (8)	Worried (8) Resentful (6) Irritated (6)

A good time to record your thoughts is when you notice a change in your mood. Look back to what was running through your mind immediately beforehand and try to jot down your thoughts straight away (it's easier!).

Over the course of a few days, you will become sensitive to changes in your feelings and to the thoughts that spark them off. You may well find that the same thoughts occur again and again. Then you should evaluate your thoughts to ascertain whether they are enhancing your success or holding you back.

But before you get to that stage, let's practise completing a Thought Record.

Making appointments

Take an example from your day-to-day activity, such as setting up appointments with prospective clients. Think back to the last time you had a run of negative replies. Do a mental action-replay (if it helps, close your eyes). What was the situation? When? Where? With whom? What were you feeling? What was going through your mind about it?

Complete the Thought Record on page 48. (You may want to photocopy this beforehand to ensure that you have enough of them.) Rate how strongly you believed each of your thought(s) on a 0–10 scale and rate the strength of your feeling(s) on the same scale.

Here are some hints you might find useful.

Hint 1: Automatic thoughts often have silent words – such as 'all', 'always', 'never' – lurking out of sight. You need to look for these words in your thoughts and write them on the Thought Record.

Hint 2: Often our thoughts come as questions. It's important to change these questions into statements on your Thought Record. For example, if one of your thoughts is 'What if I can't manage it?', you could change this to 'I won't be able to manage it' because that is what you are *really* thinking.

Hint 3: Match the strength of your thoughts with the strength of your feelings. For instance, if you rate your belief that a client is interested in buying your product or service at 8 out of 10, then you'd feel hopeful at the same rating.

Hint 4: Feelings are usually expressed in one word – for example, excited, nervous, happy, fearful.

Once you have filled in the Thought Record above, ask yourself:

• How did you respond to that situation?

• Did your response match the thoughts you had?

Now try another example.

Referrals

Think back to the last time you were about to ask a client for a referred lead. Again, carry out a mental action-replay. What was the situation? When? Where? With whom? Doing what? What was going through your mind beforehand?

Complete another Thought Record. Once you have done this, ask yourself:

• How did I respond to that situation?

• Did my response correspond with my thoughts?

Now review what you have jotted down on your Thought Records. You should find that a basic factor in how you respond to a particular situation is the way in which you interpret that situation.

Are your thoughts enhancing your success?

So far, you have learned how to recognize your automatic thoughts. This is the first important step in the 'four steps to success' (see page 9).

Situation	Thoughts (Rate how much you believe each thought; scale 0–10)	Feelings (Rate strength 0–10)

The second step is to judge whether your thoughts lead to helpful feelings and ways of behaving. And third, if your thoughts are unhelpful, you have to learn how to substitute more effective ways of thinking in order to feel better and do better. Then you practise the new ways of thinking until they become habits.

Let's take **stress** as an example. All jobs have elements of stress. It is often caused by things in our environment – events, interactions with people, etc. – and can be a very realistic response to the particular situation. After all, it would be quite legitimate to feel stress if someone threatens to hit you! However, stress can also be caused by our thoughts or our interpretation of a situation. For instance, stress is a common response to the scenario on page 4 (waiting for a friend in a restaurant).

There are a number of ways of reducing stress. One is to work on the feelings produced by the stress once they have occurred (e.g. by yoga, relaxation courses, having a drink or two), but this can be inconvenient, difficult or, in the case of alcohol, unhealthy. Another way is to eliminate or modify the *source* of the stress. However, there will always be some sources of stress that we cannot change.

A third way to reduce stress is to recognize the powerful role that your thoughts play in determining how you feel. **Stress can be reduced by changing how you think.** It's a case of ascertaining what you are thinking about a particular situation, and if needed, use some of the strategies I'm about to introduce to you in order to take a different perspective.

The following two exercises illustrate how a change in thinking can influence how much stress you feel.

Imagine this scenario. You have borrowed your partner's brand-new car, which is his/her pride and joy and for which he/she saved for years to buy. You have run into a post and dented the car badly. You are now on your way home and are dreading telling him/her. You don't feel like going home.

On the form below, make a list of stress-producing thoughts, those that would get your stress level right up. Write down as many as you can, then rate how much stress you would feel on a 0–10 scale. Next, write down a list of stress-reducing thoughts, those that would go some way towards reducing the stress you'd feel. Then rate the stress felt from these thoughts on a 0–10 scale.

The car crash scenario	
Situation: You have dented your partner's brand-new car. You are now on your way home and are dreading telling him/her.	
Stress-producing thoughts:	Stress-reducing thoughts:
Stress (0–10)	Stress (0–10)

Now let's take a second example. You don't get a bonus that you had been hoping for. You have already mentally spent it: you had been looking forward to a holiday and had promised your children a video game set. You are feeling very disappointed.

Write down some stress-producing thoughts and then some stress-reducing ones. Rate how much stress you'd feel from each set of thoughts.

The bonus scenario

Situation: You don't get a bonus that you had been hoping for.

Stress-producing thoughts:	Stress-reducing thoughts:
Stress (0–10)	**Stress (0–10)**

As you completed each exercise, you should have found that stress was reduced by changing your thoughts about the event, that is, by getting a different perspective on it. The event itself did not change – all that changed was your thinking.

Now let's see if we can apply this technique to a real situation. Think of a difficult situation you are currently facing. Describe it briefly in the box below. Next, write a list of stress-producing thoughts, and then a list of thoughts that will reduce your stress. Rate on a scale of 0–10 the amount of stress you would feel with each set of thoughts. Be realistic!

Personal situation	
Situation:	
Stress-producing thoughts:	**Stress-reducing thoughts:**
Stress (0–10)	**Stress (0–10)**

Did you find that you were able to change the level of the stress that you were feeling by changing your thoughts about the situation? How did you do it? If you were to advise someone else to change their thoughts, what strategy would you recommend?

We'll return to this question in a minute.

Common thinking errors

There are a number of common thinking distortions that people make when feeling stressed or demotivated. These 'thinking errors' are common – everyone has them to some degree – but they can undermine your effectiveness. It is important, therefore, to be aware of your thinking errors, so that you can gain control over them.

We each have our 'favourite' thinking errors – that is, the ones that we tend to use frequently. See if you can recognize any that you use, in the list below, adapted from D. D. Burns' book *The Feeling Good Handbook* (New York, Penguin Books, 1990).

- **All-or-nothing thinking** You see everything in only two categories: black or white. For example, if you don't do something perfectly, you tell yourself that you've failed. You must work hard all the time or else you will tell yourself that you're lazy. Unless your clothes are immaculate, you tell yourself that you're scruffy. All-or-nothing thinking forms the basis of perfectionism.

- **Jumping to conclusions** You jump to a negative conclusion when there is hardly any or no evidence to support your conclusion. You might also find yourself mind-reading – that is, assuming that you know what other people are thinking without first checking out your hunches. For example, you've heard some rumours about redundancies coming up at work, and when your manager calls you in for a meeting, you think: 'This is it, he's going to tell me I've been made redundant.'

- **Magnification (catastrophizing) or minimization** You magnify your problems and imperfections. Negative things that are just remote possibilities become definites in your mind, and you believe that they will end up as catastrophes. At the same time, you minimize your strengths, resources and ability to cope with problems. For instance, you've been asked to rewrite a large order and you think: 'This is terrible. I'll never get my bonus now.'

- **Emotional reasoning** You take your emotions as evidence of the truth: I feel it, therefore it must be true. For example, 'I feel guilty, therefore I must have done something bad,' or 'I feel overwhelmed, therefore my workload must be impossible to tackle.'

- **'Should' statements** You set very high standards for yourself and tell yourself that you should do this and ought to do that: 'I should work hard in my job and not take time off' or 'I ought to work late to finish this work.' You feel very guilty if you fall short of your 'shoulds' and 'oughts'. You might also set high standards for other people and then feel resentful if they don't measure up.

- **Labelling and mislabelling** Instead of describing your effort factually, you attach a negative label to yourself:

'I'm a failure' rather than 'I made a mistake.' When someone else's behaviour rubs you the wrong way, you attach a negative label to him or her: 'He's an uncooperative egotist.' Labelling involves describing an event with language that is highly coloured and emotionally loaded.

Did you recognize yourself in any of these thinking errors? In the box below, make a note of the thinking errors you are most likely to employ and give examples of when they might happen. Identify the one you tend to use most often and mark it with a cross.

The thinking errors I use most

1

2

3

Now see if you can identify the thinking errors in the following situation. Barry, a highly experienced and successful tele-sales consultant, loses a large sale that he had been very optimistic about. He is extremely disappointed, having promised the family a holiday from the commission.

He thinks to himself:

- I should have got that one.
- If I can't close a sale like that, I'll never make it in this business.
- My manager will think I'm losing my touch.
- Who would think of promoting me now?
- They say the economy is in recession, but I'm sure it's just me.

Write any thinking errors you find against each of Barry's thoughts. The answers are provided for you at the end of this chapter.

When you've done that, I want to make a wager with you. (I always win this bet, so I'm on safe ground here.) Go back to the car crash and bonus scenarios and look at the stress-producing thoughts in each one. I'll bet that you'll find many thinking errors in the stress-producing thoughts. In fact, that is why such thoughts *are* stress-producing: they are full of thinking errors. In each case, label the thinking errors you find.

Next revisit the stress-producing thoughts in your personal stress example (page 52). See if you can find any thinking errors there and label them, too.

How did you go? Did I win my bet? Did you find any thinking errors?

Conclusion

That brings us to the end of Stage 3. We've worked on a method for tuning into thinking by recording thoughts, and we've made a start on ways to ascertain whether thoughts are helpful, by checking to see if they contain any thinking errors. In Stage 4, I'll show you how to change unhelpful thinking to enhance your chances of success.

Next week's tasks

1 During the next week, complete a Thought Record about two different situations, one positive and one negative. Note when you are experiencing a particular mood and 'catch' the thoughts that are causing that mood. On the Thought Record, briefly outline the situation, your thoughts (rating each one from 0 to 10 according to how much you believed it) and the resulting mood or feelings (rated for intensity).

Try to complete the Thought Records during the actual situation in which the thoughts occur. If this is not possible, note your thoughts on a piece of paper as soon as you can.

2 Catch your thinking errors! Throughout the week, identify your thinking errors (especially the one you pinpointed as using most often) and note them on the form overleaf. At the end of each day, tally up the number of thinking errors you've 'caught'. You'll probably find that the more thinking errors you've had, the worse you've felt (pessimistic, stressed, demotivated, angry, etc.).

3 Using the Weekly Plan and weekly Prospecting Register (*overleaf*), outline your plan of activity for next week. Make sure there is a good balance of activities including some of your personal motivating activities, some speculative approaches to potential clients and a further step towards one of your goals.

Day	Thinking error	Tally

Weekly Plan

Week beginning ....../....../......

	......day	......day	......day	......day	......day	......day	......day
AM							
PM							
Evening							

Prospecting Register

Client/ Prospect	Current Business	Canvass Details	Outcome	Cause of the Outcome

4 Complete the third week's entry in your Personal Log (page 162): 'Something I have learned (about myself, my job, etc.) which I will find useful.'

Answers to 'Can you identify the thinking errors?' (page 56): 'should' statement, all-or-nothing thinking, jumping to conclusions, magnifying (catastrophizing), all-or-nothing thinking.

Challenging Your Thoughts

Do you have days like this?

It starts off badly at home with an argument with your partner. When you arrive at the office, your manager is just leaving, but he indicates on his way out that he wants to see you in his office at 9am tomorrow. Your sales figures yesterday were disastrous, and when you meet your colleagues in the office, you learn that they all had an excellent day and have brought in several sales each.

You and the team do a telephone appointment session together. They all make at least five or six appointments for next week before leaving for their client appointments for the day. You've been unable to make any appointments despite having made 20 calls.

The administration clerk hands you a note saying that two of your appointments for today have been cancelled. You spend the afternoon sorting through your paperwork without making any appreciable progress.

What would you be thinking as you drive home? How would you feel?

Difficulties, frustrations and setbacks are common in selling. Some people skip around the hurdles, others tackle them the hard way and still others lose faith in their abilities and give up.

What is important is not that difficulties give rise to self-doubts – that is a natural reaction – but how quickly you bounce back after encountering these difficulties. It all depends on your thinking.

Let's take a different situation.

Say you've been cultivating a very large sale for many months. The clients have been to see you a number of times, and you know that they are interested. You've gone to a lot of extra effort for them – getting additional information, sending off for samples, negotiating a special deal with head office on their behalf. Today is the day they're coming in to sign on the dotted line.

However, when they arrive, the clients indicate, contrary to your expectations, that they want to activate only half of the sale now, but in six months they want to take the remainder and much more, and they'd like you to do it all for them. Strangely, you feel quite deflated. You can't be bothered to work on anything else and end up wasting the entire afternoon.

Again, it's all to do with your thinking. Even positive situations can result in thoughts that undermine personal effectiveness.

So how can you improve your thinking in order to enhance your success?

Thought challenging

The answer lies in a process called 'thought challenging'. It consists of testing your thoughts against the evidence and looking for alternative views. It's as if you're taking your thoughts to court and cross-examining them.

There are a number of ways of doing this, but my research has shown that four strategies are key to enhancing success. I'll show you step-by-step how to challenge your thoughts using these techniques.

It's easiest to learn how to do it on a Thought Record. You've used a three-column Thought Record; now we're going to extend it to five columns (page 65).

You start the same way as before by noting what the situation was, your thoughts about it (and how much you believed each thought), and the feelings or behaviour that resulted from your thoughts (don't forget to rate the feelings 0–10). Next you choose the thought that has had the most effect on your mood; this is usually the one with the highest rating. Draw a circle around it.

Then in the fourth column, you challenge each of your thoughts in turn, starting with the strongest thought. To do this, you ask yourself the Four Challenging Questions, listed below. The fifth column is used to record your *new* feelings and behaviour after you've challenged your thoughts.

The Four Challenging Questions

Question 1: Am I making any thinking errors?

Let's take Jane's situation as an example. A marketing manager in a multinational company, she's been invited to put together a large proposal for a very lucrative consultancy contract with a client organisation. However, she's encountered a number of problems along the way and has been unable to submit the proposal. She thinks to herself: 'I

Situation	Thoughts (0–10)	Feelings (0–10)	Challenge thoughts	New feelings (0–10)

haven't got what it takes any more' (which she believes 7 out of 10); 'I should have anticipated these problems' (9); and 'I've let down both my boss and the company' (8). She feels very despondent (8).

Use the list on page 53 to check Jane's thoughts for thinking errors.

Did you spot the all-or-nothing thinking, a 'should' statement and jumping to conclusions?

So, the first challenging question you should ask yourself is: 'Am I making any thinking errors?'

Question 2: *What is the evidence for and against my thoughts?*

Here you ask: 'What are the facts?' It's important to remember that our thoughts are *not* facts – they are ideas or hunches – and, therefore, it's possible for them to be distorted. That's why we need to collect evidence, just like in a court case.

Often, finding evidence to support our thoughts is easy – we've had lots of practice doing this – and at the same time, we've become adept at overlooking evidence against them. But it's important to ask yourself: 'Is there *100% evidence* for these thoughts? And is there any evidence *against* them?'

Take a look at the evidence Jane came up with when she cross-examined her thought: 'I haven't got what it takes any more.'

For: 'I didn't get the proposal submitted.'

Against: 'I've been doing this job well for ten years and this is the first deadline I've missed. I've won other contracts for the company. I have good consultancy skills and I know my area well. I got an excellent appraisal this year.'

To recap, a second way to challenge your thoughts is to ask: What is the evidence for and against these thoughts?

Question 3: *What are other ways of looking at this situation?*

Often we seize on one view of a situation without considering others. For instance, Jane's automatic thought was: 'I haven't got what it takes any more.' Notice that this explanation implies that the outcome was *wholly* determined by Jane. However, there is usually not just one view of a situation. Typically, many things contribute to an outcome.

Jane needs to ask herself what other factors are likely to be contributing to this particular outcome. One way that she can do this is to imagine her thoughts as pieces of a pie.*

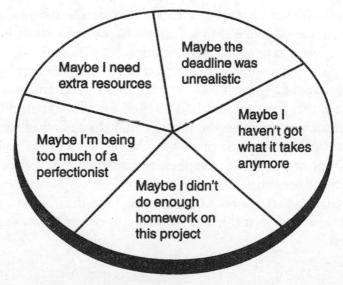

*Adapted from *Optimism ABC* by Dr M. E. P. Seligman and Foresight Inc.

Jane's automatic thought – 'I haven't got what it takes any more' – is one possible view of the situation. But instead of it being the *only* view – that is, the whole pie – it becomes just one slice of it. Jane then needs to look for other ways of viewing the situation – other slices of the pie.

The idea is to try to fill up the whole pie with alternatives – they're all just possibilities at this stage. It helps if you start with 'Maybe …'

Just thinking about alternatives can help us to regain our positive focus. But we need to continue checking out the evidence for each possibility. This is where the next challenging question comes in.

Question 4: What action can I take?

Here you devise ways to check out your alternative ideas or, if the evidence shows that your automatic thought *is* true, ways to deal with the situation.

Jane spoke with her manager and colleagues to get hard facts about her performance and about other tricky contracts that the company had pitched for. She also decided to seek advice about the strategy that she had used when putting together this proposal. On the basis of the information she received, she decided to change her approach with future proposals.

So these are the Four Challenging Questions. They help to fine-tune your thinking in order to enhance your success.

The Four Challenging Questions

1 Am I making any thinking errors?

2 What is the evidence? What are the facts?

3 What alternative views are there?

4 What action can I take?

Having challenged your thoughts, you then record your new feelings in the fifth column and rate how strong they are. Some of these feelings may be the same as the previous ones you had but are now not as strong (if they were unhelpful feelings), or you may have completely new feelings.

As a result of challenging her thoughts, Jane reduced her demoralized feelings to 4 out of 10 and regained her feelings of confidence (8) and self-belief (7).

The aim of the Four Challenging Questions is to test the validity of your thoughts and to reduce any unhelpful feelings and behaviour they may cause. This is important for positive situations as well as negative ones. Although it may be more difficult to see, positive thoughts of a particular type can also undermine your success. I'll return to this point later.

Now, I'm going to make another bet with you. Take another look at the stress-producing and stress-reducing thoughts that you imagined could have occurred in the car crash and bonus scenarios on pp. 50–1. You will find

A. Situation	B. Thoughts	C. Feelings	D. Challenge thoughts	E. New feelings
Jane didn't get a proposal submitted	I haven't got what it takes any more (7). I should have anticipated these problems (9). I've let down both my boss and the company (8).	Despondent (8)	*Thinking errors:* all-or-nothing thinking, a 'should' statement and jumping to conclusions *Evidence* *For:* I didn't get the proposal submitted. *Against:* I've been doing this job well for ten years. This is the first deadline I've missed. I've won other contracts for the company. I have good consultancy skills and I know my area well. I got an excellent appraisal this year. *Alternatives* Maybe I haven't got what it takes. Maybe the deadline was unrealistic. Maybe I didn't do enough homework on this project. Maybe I needed extra resources. Maybe I'm being too much of a perfectionistic *Action* Speak with manager and colleagues. Seek advice about strategy.	Despondent (4) Confidence (8) Self-belief (7)

that, by changing the thoughts from stress-producing to stress-reducing, you used one or more of the Four Challenging Questions. See if you can spot them. Write the challenging question used – thinking error, evidence, alternative, action – in the margin against the various stress-reducing thoughts.

The Four Challenging Questions transform unhelpful thinking into positive, powerful thinking. I'll be asking you to try them out on some of your own thoughts, but first try this example.

The silent assessor

Situation
It's the last day of an important course and you're being assessed. At lunchtime, you meet the course assessor on the way to the bar. He acknowledges you and then doesn't speak to you for the rest of the way. He joins another group of people at the bar.

Thoughts
• He's displeased with me.
• He doesn't like me.
• I've failed the course.

Feelings
You feel tense (9), concerned (9) and dejected (5).

Task: Use the Four Challenging Questions to help combat these stress-producing thoughts and reduce the negative feelings so that you'll be able to perform well in the exam during the afternoon.

1 Thinking errors

2 Evidence

3 Alternatives

4 Action

Challenging positive thoughts

As I've already mentioned, the Four Challenging Questions are useful to test your thoughts about positive situations as well as negative ones.

Let's go back to the situation on page 63 at the beginning of this chapter. The client has committed to part of the sale now and significantly more in six months' time. This is a positive situation, yet even positive situations can result in thoughts that undermine personal effectiveness.

In the space below, write down some of the automatic thoughts that are likely to have produced the feelings of deflation in this situation.

....
....
....
....
....
....

Next we need to challenge those thoughts using the Four Challenging Questions.

In the following Thought Record, I have included some ideas for the above example, using the Four Challenging Questions. There are no right or wrong answers; the key is to come up with as many different ideas as possible. Complete the three further examples, and in each case ascertain what feelings the thought would create, then cross-examine the thoughts to produce new feelings.

Thought Record

A. Situation	B. Thoughts (rate 0–10)	C. Feelings (rate 0–10)	D. Evaluate and challenge thoughts	E. New feelings (rate 0–10)
A client has committed to part of a large sale now and much more in six months' time.	I should have been able to close that sale completely (8). I must be losing my touch (7). They'll probably change their mind and cancel the future business (6).	Deflated (7)	*Thinking errors* 'Should' statement. Jumping to conclusions *Evidence* For: The client didn't commit to the whole package. Against: They have indicated that they want more in the future. They've specifically asked me to work with them. I have achieved a significant sale even if it's not the whole lot. *Alternatives* Maybe they will change their mind and cancel the rest of the order. Maybe they will take the future order. Maybe I'll be able to lever additional business from them. Maybe I'll be able to get some referred leads from them. *Action* Keep in touch with the client and look for ways to meet their needs.	Deflated (2) Motivated (8) Pleased (6)

74

A. Situation	B. Thoughts (rate 0–10)	C. Feelings (rate 0–10)	D. Evaluate and challenge thoughts	E. New feelings (rate 0–10)
A colleague who started on the same day as you has made four large sales and you've only made one small one.	This counts for nothing – it's the big ones I want (7). I should be doing better (6).		*Thinking errors* *Evidence* *For* *Against* *Alternatives* *Action*	

A. Situation	B. Thoughts (rate 0–10)	C. Feelings (rate 0–10)	D. Evaluate and challenge thoughts	E. New feelings (rate 0–10)
My manager has suggested that I increase my personal production.	I can't do that amount of business (9). Why me (5)? I'm already working at full capacity (8).		*Thinking errors* *Evidence* *For* *Against* *Alternatives* *Action*	

A. Situation	B. Thoughts (rate 0–10)	C. Feelings (rate 0–10)	D. Evaluate and challenge thoughts	E. New feelings (rate 0–10)
You've closed a big sale and are being congratulated by your colleagues.	They're just being pleasant (7). The senior consultant actually sold it to my client (8). It didn't have anything to do with me (5).		*Thinking errors* *Evidence* *For* *Against* *Alternatives* *Action*	

Now it's your turn. Think of two personal examples – one a recent success, the other a difficult experience you've encountered recently, which you think that you responded to in an ineffective manner (e.g. a disagreement with someone, a poor decision made).

Using the Thought Record overleaf, write down your thoughts about each of these two situations in turn. Write as many thoughts as you can. Don't forget to look for silent words in your thoughts and change any questions into statements. Rate each thought on a scale of 1 to 10, then circle the strongest thought. Write your feelings in the C column and rate them out of 10 as well.

Now you're ready to ask yourself the Four Challenging Questions. Challenge each of your thoughts in turn, starting with the strongest one. Decide whether some or all of these thoughts could be changed so that they would be more helpful. For instance, you might decide to take more credit for your successes.

1 'Am I making any thinking errors?' Use the list of thinking errors on page 53 to help you.

2 'What is the evidence? Is there 100% evidence *for* my thought? Is there any evidence *against* it?'

3 'What are some other ways of looking at the situation? If I were another person, how might I see the situation?' Write down as many possibilities as you can. Try starting your thoughts with 'Maybe ...'

4 What actions can I take to deal with the situation or to check out my alternative views?' Make a list of these actions.

Thought Record

A. Situation	B. Thoughts (rate 0–10)	C. Feelings (rate 0–10)	D. Evaluate and challenge thoughts	E. New feelings (rate 0–10)

How did you do with that exercise? Which of the Four Challenging Questions did you find easiest to use? Were you able to change your feelings as a result of challenging your thoughts?

Common mistakes

Challenging your thoughts is certainly the key to success in selling. But there are some common mistakes to watch out for. Forewarned is forearmed!

Mistake 1

One mistake that people commonly make is trying to challenge thoughts that are questions. For instance, in the B column of your Thought Record, you might have written: 'How am I going to manage if the client gets upset when I tell him that I've undercharged him?'

You need to change the question into a statement – such as 'I won't be able to manage if he gets upset' – because you can't challenge a question, and also because the latter thought is probably what you are really thinking deep down.

Mistake 2

A second common mistake is replacing unhelpful thoughts with empty positive thinking.

Consider this example. Say you needed to work on some urgent paperwork one evening, but you were feeling very unmotivated. Your thoughts were: 'I'm too tired to do it. I'd rather watch TV. I've become lazy.' You challenged these thoughts with 'I can do it. As soon as I get up out of the chair, I'll feel fine.' But it made no difference. You felt just as unmotivated as before and ended up doing nothing all evening.

This challenge is an example of empty positive thinking. Wishing something to be the case will not change how you feel and act. To turbo-charge your performance, your new thoughts need to be realistic and believable. That's what makes *Successful Selling*'s challenging techniques different from other tools on the market.

Mistake 3

A third common mistake in thought challenging is when you don't tap into *all* your thoughts. Sometimes there are further thoughts beneath the surface, and these are the real cause of your feelings or behaviour. These deeper thoughts are called 'core beliefs'. They need to be uncovered and challenged to make lasting improvements to your thinking and performance.

We'll be looking at the fascinating subject of core beliefs in Stage 4. But before we move on to that, check back over the thought challenging that you did earlier and make sure that you didn't make any of the common mistakes outlined above.

Conclusion

OK, that brings us to the end of this stage. In it, we've focused on four techniques that have been proven to enhance success in selling: the Four Challenging Questions. Don't worry if you weren't able to change your feelings when you first used them, or if they felt a bit awkward; this is quite normal at the outset. Through my research with sales people, I've found that the more they practise these techniques, the more adept they become at challenging their thoughts (to the extent that they can do it in their heads after a while). And the better they are at cross-examining their thoughts, the more they are able to bounce back after problems and achieve peak performance.

Next week's tasks

1 In preparation for the next stage, think back over the past twelve months and select four successes that you have had. In the box opposite, briefly outline each success and write down its cause.

2 Try this experiment. Choose a task that you're not particularly looking forward to this week. (It might be the approaches to potential clients that you put into your plan for this week.) Before starting the task, ascertain what you think about it and write your thoughts on the Thought Record on page 84.

Now carry out a courtroom cross-examination. Use the Four Challenging Questions to test your thoughts and, if warranted, modify them to make them more productive, positive and powerful. After you've done this, carry out the task and make a note of any differences that there might have been.

3 Weekly plan
Again plan your activity for the next week, this time including five prospecting approaches and five requests for referred leads.

Successes	Causes
1	1
2	2
3	3
4	4

Thought Record

A. Situation	B. Thoughts (rate 0–10)	C. Feelings (rate 0–10)	D. Evaluate and challenge negative thoughts	E. New feelings (rate 0–10)

Ensure that your week contains a good balance of activities, including personal motivating activities, a further step on your chosen goal (page 21) and, of course, at least one reward.

If you are reluctant to engage in any of these activities, tap into your thoughts about them to see if you can find out why you would like to avoid them. Then challenge your thoughts to see if they are backed up by good, hard evidence.

4 Complete the fourth week's entry in your Personal Log: 'Something I have learned (about myself, my job, etc.) which I will find useful.'

Weekly Plan

Week beginning ....../....../......

	......day	......day	......day	......day	......day	......day	......day
AM							
PM							
Evening							

Prospecting Register

Client/ Prospect	Current Business	Canvass Details	Outcome	Cause of the Outcome

Stage 5:

Core Beliefs

Have you ever wondered what makes you react to situations the way you do? Perhaps you've noticed that, without consciously thinking about it, you tend to repeat certain patterns of behaviour, some of which are helpful and others that perhaps are not so helpful? These patterns of behaviour are the result of thought habits that each of us has developed over the years. For example, do you know people who always seem to take control, or those who continually do things to please others? Behaviours such as these stem from their core beliefs.

Each of us has many different core beliefs about the ways things are or the way things should be. They are deeply held and determine how we think and act.

Core beliefs are like the roots of a tree – fundamental to its life and its healthy functioning, but usually hidden beneath the surface. The leaves of the tree are our automatic thoughts. They flutter in the wind and can be hard to catch, but you *can* see them. However, the leaves of a tree are fed by its roots. Similarly, our core beliefs feed our automatic thoughts, influence our behaviour and regulate how we experience the world.

Core beliefs play a useful role. They provide 'rules' that guide us in the way we think, feel and act. They also allow

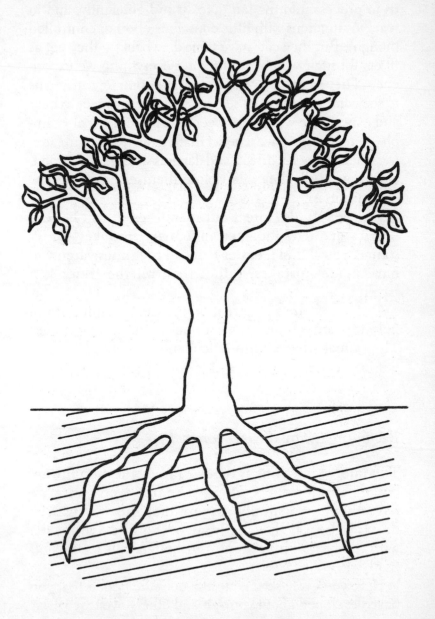

us to process information quickly and efficiently, and to react to situations with little conscious effort or controlled thought. But they can have their drawbacks – they act as filters through which we interpret everything we experience. They influence what we pay attention to, causing us to see what we expect to see, hear what we expect to hear and experience what we expect to experience. For example, some people have a belief that the world is a threatening place. They see threats and dangers where others don't, and as a result, they often close themselves off to new opportunities.

Our beliefs also affect our memories. If you believe that it's shameful for a person to make mistakes, for instance, you'll find it easier to recall the times when you have made mistakes, rather than all the times you haven't.

Our core beliefs – correct or incorrect, helpful or unhelpful – are the source of our behaviour and attitudes. They affect what we think, feel and do – and how successful we are.

Becoming aware of your core beliefs

The interesting thing is that we rarely question the accuracy of our beliefs; often we're not even aware we have them. We simply assume that the way we see things is the way they really are or should be. But even with the best of intentions, our beliefs can lead us off track.

Have you ever asked yourself about the beliefs that you have developed about yourself and others over the years?

How do they affect what you do? Are they enhancing your success or are they holding you back?

To make quantum improvements in your performance, you need to get to work on the roots – the beliefs from which your attitudes and behaviour grow.

The first step is to become aware of them. Here are some core beliefs that others have uncovered:

- if I work as part of a team, I'll be more successful;

- unless I do what I commit myself to do, I'll feel less of a person;

- you should always put other people first;

- if I ask for help, it's a sign of weakness;

- unless I'm useful, productive or creative, life is boring;

- if I don't prepare well, I'm less effective;

- if I treat other people with fairness and respect, the world will be a better place;

- if I make mistakes, I look stupid;

- if I'm not in charge of my own destiny, I can't be happy;

- I should be able to excel at everything I try.

Later, I'm going to suggest that you write down some of your core beliefs, but before you do, let's look a little further at each of the core beliefs above.

What automatic thoughts and what types of behaviour do you think might result from each of these beliefs? Take each belief in turn and imagine what thoughts or behaviour a person would be likely to exhibit with that core belief. I've done the first one for you.

Core belief	Associated thoughts and behaviour
Unless I do what I commit myself to do, I'll feel less of a person.	Avoids taking on anything much at all, for fear of not being able to deliver.
If I work as part of a team, I'll be more successful.	
You should always put other people first.	
If I ask for help, it's a sign of weakness.	
Unless I'm useful, productive or creative, life is boring.	
If I don't prepare well, I'm less effective.	
If I treat other people with fairness and respect, the world will be a better place.	
If I make mistakes, I look stupid.	
If I'm not in charge of my own destiny, I can't be happy.	
I should be able to excel at everything I try.	

It's important to remember with core beliefs that many are positive and helpful and serve a valuable role in our lives. For example, 'If I treat people with fairness and respect, the world will be a better place' is a sound belief to hold.

Other core beliefs may have been helpful in the past, but may now need to be updated. An example of this type of belief might be: 'I must be excellent in all areas – and be able to prove it.' This is perhaps a useful belief to have when you are competing for a university place, but in terms of building a good sales business, it gets in the way.

Still other beliefs may actually be destructive, undermining our effectiveness, well-being and/or our relationships with others. These are usually inflexible or exaggerated, often the sacred cows that we don't even question. One salesperson with whom I once worked had a deeply held belief: 'If I fail, it means I'm incompetent and I've let others down.' You can imagine how it was holding him back in his business (and making him very miserable, too).

The more we are aware of our beliefs, the more we can examine them, test them against reality and, if necessary, change them to enhance personal effectiveness and our quality of life.

So now let's turn to *your* core beliefs. What are the core beliefs (the 'rules' or 'truths') that you have developed about yourself, the world and others? Write some of them in the box below. Notice, from the examples above, that core beliefs are usually written as 'If ... then ...' statements: 'If this, then that.' They also come as 'shoulds' or 'musts'.

My core beliefs
1
2
3
4
5

If you had trouble with this activity, be reassured that it is not always easy to recognize your core beliefs. Nevertheless it *is* important to try. To attain higher performance levels, you need to uncover your beliefs, take a good look at them and decide whether they still serve your best interests.

Here are three techniques to help you do this.

1 *Look for repeating themes or patterns in your thoughts*

Like a toothache, core beliefs often come back to nag you. Here is an example:

A. Situation	B. Thoughts	C. Feelings
Looking at the new weekly return system	This needs to be done meticulously. I have to see a client in an hour, so I had better not start working on it now.	Stressed (8)
Checking a quotation before sending it off	Oh no! There's a typing error. The whole thing will have to be done again. I couldn't possibly send it off with an error.	Irritated (7)
Examining the work of a decorator	He's missed a bit behind the dresser. What a shoddy job. If something is worth doing, it's worth doing well.	Irritated (6)

Can you spot the theme in the above thoughts? Which of the following do you think it is?

Fear of not being in control ☐
Needing to do things perfectly ☐
Being unloveable ☐
Fear of looking stupid ☐

Yes, there's a theme of perfectionism running through this Thought Record.

Now, check your own Thought Record in Stage 4 – are there any themes or patterns in your thoughts?

2 Look for the emotional charge

Another way a core belief can show itself is through the emotional charge it carries. People talk of 'touching a raw nerve' or 'erupting like a volcano' – when a person's mood or behaviour is much more extreme than the situation warrants. It is a good indication that a core belief has been triggered.

Let me give you an example. Julia was preparing for a very important presentation to a large client company when she discovered that one member of the sales team had, without telling her, changed a course of action that had been previously agreed with the client. Julia was furious. She told off the team member in no uncertain terms, phoned the client and postponed the sales presentation.

Which of the following core beliefs do you think this situation might have triggered in Julia?

If I work as part of a team, I'll be more successful. ☐

If I disagree with someone, they won't respect me. ☐

Unless I'm in control, I can't be effective.   ☐

Yes, you're right – it's the last one. Julia's reaction far outweighed what the situation warranted. The incident triggered one of her core beliefs.

If you've had a strong emotional reaction to something, you've probably triggered one of your core beliefs. Can you think of an occasion when this has happened to you? Which of your core beliefs do you think you may have triggered?

3 Use the 'downward arrow' technique

This involves working backwards from your automatic thoughts until you come to one of your core beliefs. You take each of your automatic thoughts and ask yourself the question: 'What does this thought mean to me?'

What does the thought mean about you, about other people, about the world? With each new thought you come up with, ask yourself the same question again: 'What does *this* thought mean to me?'

It's like going from the leaves of a tree back down the branches, all the way down the trunk to the ground and then into the roots. You keep going down until you find the end of the root. This is your core belief.

Here's an example. David had finally sat down to tackle the paperwork that had been building up over the last few weeks. He felt extremely fed up, but he was at a loss to understand why. So he used the 'downward arrow' technique to see if there were any further thoughts lurking

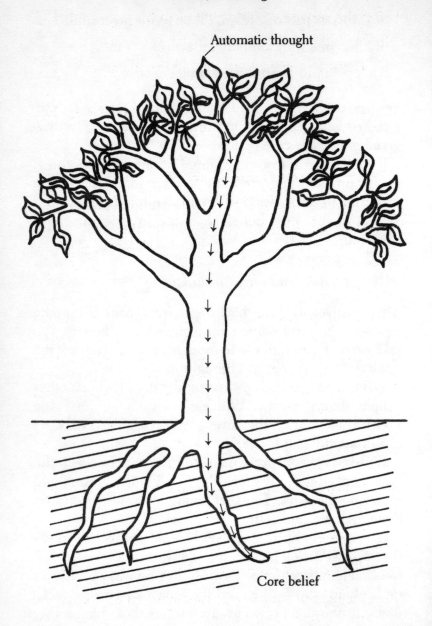

Automatic thought

Core belief

below the surface that might explain his negative mood. This is what he came up with.

> *Thought*: 'I can't cope with all this paperwork.'
> *What does that mean to me?*

> *Thought*: 'Paperwork is an important aspect of this job.'
> *What does that mean to me?*

> *Thought*: 'It means I'm not coping with the job.'
> *What does that mean to me?*

> *Thought*: 'Unless I'm fully in control of every aspect of the job, I'm never going to be a top salesperson.'

This last thought – David's core belief – is clearly the cause of his mood, and it's pulling him down. He now needs to challenge it.

Consider another example. Ron is driving to a client appointment. He's behind a series of cars waiting to over-take a slow-moving lorry. Suddenly a sporty car driven by a young man overtakes him and slips into the gap, causing Ron to brake suddenly. Momentarily he feels angry, but then he feels quite depressed.

> *Thought*: 'Look at him! Impatient fool.'
> *What does that mean to me?*

> *Thought*: 'He ought to be fined for dangerous driving.'
> *What does that mean to me?*

> *Thought*: 'I should have seen him coming and closed the gap.'
> *What does that mean to me?*

> *Thought*: 'If I can't outmanoeuvre young fools on the road, I'm no longer up to it.'

The thought causing Ron's mood was the last one, his core belief, rather than the automatic thought that first popped into his head.

Core beliefs need to be uncovered and checked to see if they are helpful. And if they're unhelpful, they need to be challenged so that you can make lasting changes to your thinking and actions. Let me show you, step-by-step, how to do this.

Unpack your thoughts

Chose a situation you wish to analyse. It might be one in which you were unable to understand your reaction fully, or one in which your thought-challenging didn't work too well. Using the form on page 102, set down all your thoughts in the left-hand column. Don't forget to look for silent words in your thoughts and write them down, too. Also change any questions into statements.

Next, circle the thought with the highest rating (the one with the greatest effect on your mood) and write it at the top of the middle column. Then use the 'downward arrow' technique to uncover – or 'unpack' – your core belief. Ask yourself 'What does that thought mean to me?' until you can't go any further down the root of the tree.

Test your core beliefs

Having come up with your core belief, the next step is to challenge it to see whether it is realistic. Using the Four Challenging Questions, cross-examine your belief.

- First, check whether there are any thinking errors in your belief.

- Next, look at the evidence. Often we treat our core beliefs as absolute facts. We use them as indisputable rules to guide our lives, and we overlook evidence that shows that they're not 100% true all of the time. Is there 100% evidence to support your core belief? Is there any evidence *against* it? Treat your core belief as if it might be true but just as equally might be false. Write any evidence *against* your core belief in the right-hand column on the form, and during the week, see if you can find any more evidence against it.

- The next step is to develop an alternative to your core belief: perhaps a more flexible belief or a more helpful one. Here are examples of helpful alternatives to some of the core beliefs on page 91.

    - My own opinion of myself is most important.

    - It's OK to make mistakes. They are opportunities to learn.

    - I work hard to succeed.

    - I do many things well.

    - It's a sign of good problem-solving ability to ask for help when it's needed.

    - It's not humanly possible to excel all the time.

  Ask yourself: 'What is another way of looking at my belief?' You may need to work more on this during the week.

- Action. Once you have developed your alternative belief, gather evidence for it. This may mean that you have to take some action. For example, if your core belief was that you must do things perfectly, and your alterna-

Situation:

Thoughts:

	Thinking errors
Thought...	
What does that mean to me?	
Thought...	Evidence *against* the core belief
What does that mean to me?	
Thought...	Alternative, more helpful belief
What does that mean to me?	
Thought...	Action to check out your alternative belief
What does that mean to me?	
CORE BELIEF:	

102

tive helpful belief is 'It's OK to make mistakes. They are opportunities to learn', you could try doing things less perfectly and see what happens. So thinking about your new, more helpful belief, how could you gather evidence for it? What action could you take to check it out? Write your ideas on the form.

Once you have gathered some evidence for your new core belief, the next step is to practise it. Remember, years of practice have often gone into our old core beliefs, so the new ones have to be practised too. On a daily basis, look for evidence to support your belief.

Now let's go back to the task you completed at the end of Stage 4. During the week, you were going to check your thoughts and challenge them using the Four Challenging Questions.

Check through the thoughts you have identified. Do any of them need to be 'unpacked' further? (Check for one-liners – they are a good indication that you may need to unpack further thoughts!) Are there any patterns in your thoughts? Remember, if your thought-challenging doesn't work well, or if you are unable to understand fully your reaction to a particular situation, this may be a clue that you need to look for further thought or beliefs beneath the surface.

Use the question 'What does that mean to me?' to uncover further thoughts or beliefs.

Once you have unpacked these, you then have to examine them using the Four Challenging Questions.

Analyzing core beliefs

So now, let's go back to the core beliefs you wrote on page 102. Can you add any more?

Core belief	An occasion when it has served me well	An occasion when it hasn't served me well

Once you've done that, take a few minutes to think about each core belief you've identified. Can you trace its origin? When did you pick it up? Who did you learn it from?

Now we need to take things a step further. Write down each of the core beliefs you've identified on the form overleaf. Then, for each belief, think of an occasion when it has served you well, and an occasion when it has not served you well.

Now ask yourself this question:

Do any of my beliefs need to be changed? Yes/No/Maybe
(*Please circle*)

Still using the form, let's examine this further.

• Which of your beliefs are sound and productive, necessary for your healthy functioning and personal effectiveness? Mark these with an 'R' for 'Retain'.

• Which ones need to be updated or modified? Mark those with an 'M' for 'Modify'.

• And last, which of your beliefs are unhelpful, undermining your well-being and/or your ability to achieve peak performance? Although they may be familiar and comfortable, these are the ones that you need to let go. Mark them with a 'D' for 'Discard'.

Use the techniques you've learned in this book to replace your unhelpful beliefs with more realistic alternatives. But please remember: core beliefs, particularly the problematic ones, can take longer to change than automatic thoughts. This is because we tend to overlook evidence against them – that is why they have remained unchallenged for so long. Use the Four Challenging Questions to begin to challenge them now – particularly look for evidence *against* your beliefs – and continue to do so during the next week.

Now we're going to change tack and look at successes.

Personal successes

Select one of your personal successes from the list of four you considered last week (page 83). Ask a family member or friend to interview you about your success and to list on the form below all the skills and abilities that underpinned that success.

Success:

Skills and abilities:

What did you learn from this activity?

To what did you attribute your success when you first wrote it down?

your ability? ☐

luck? ☐

the effort you had put in? ☐

the ease of the task? ☐

positive circumstances? ☐

other *(please specify)* _____

How has this changed *since* the interview? What do you now think was the *main* reason for your success? Write this down in the space provided below.

_____

_____

_____

We're going to work a lot more on successes in the next stage. In preparation for this, during the week, I'd like you to keep a diary of your successes. They don't have to be major events; small achievements are just as important as large ones. For each success, think about why it occurred.

Next week's tasks

1 Look for evidence against your unhelpful core beliefs, and evidence for the alternative, more helpful beliefs.

2 Note your successes during the week and complete the Success Diary on the following page. Look for the main reason why each success occurred.

SUCCESS DIARY

Success	Cause

3 Again plan your activity for the next week.

4 Complete the fifth week's entry in your Personal Log: 'Something I have learned (about myself, my job, etc.) which I will find useful.'

Weekly Plan

Week beginning ....../....../......

	......day	......day	......day	......day	......day	......day	......day
AM							
PM							
Evening							

Prospecting Register

Client/ Prospect	Current Business	Canvass Details	Outcome	Cause of the Outcome

Stage 6:

The Winning Formula

A case history: Mike

I had been the leading financial adviser in my district for three years running. Then there came a period between the middle of January and the middle of April when not one policy was sold in my agency, not by me nor by any of my managers. However, at the end of the year, I ended up again as the top adviser in my office.

So what happened during that awful period at the beginning of the year? Well, there were factors that were outside my control – among other things, redundancies at and possible closure of a big company we did business with – but there were also aspects that I could control. It came down to the fact that, after two or three weeks of nothing, I became almost conditioned to fail. Success breeds success, but on that occasion, failure bred failure.

I was very confused. After being successful for so long, to meet this wall of failure felt like a crushing defeat. The most disturbing thing was that I couldn't see any way round it. All I could see was that I had had three blank weeks, had nothing lined up for the next two or three weeks and, although I was getting some support from my managers, I was losing confidence in myself.

It was like looking down a dark tunnel – you knew that there must be a turn-off down there, but you couldn't see where it was.

I felt it was all down to me, and I started questioning my own actions very closely. I asked myself, having been successful in the past, was I now being too cocky, too brash? Was I not really listening? Was I just assuming that people were going to do business with me just because I wanted them to, without fully talking to them, without fully understanding and hearing what they were saying? I came to the conclusion that, yes, at the beginning of the blank period, it had been my fault to some extent. I had simply been carried along on a wave of success that had then disappeared out from under me.

It affected the rest of my work. I lost the enthusiasm I'd had for the general admin side, even though I'd previously thought of it as an essential part of the work. I lost all interest in the basic nuts and bolts of the job. And I must admit that there were some evenings when, after a couple of negative appointments, I'd throw in the towel and go home, whereas in the past, I would have happily worked until late.

On the personal side, first my earnings began to dip. Then my family suffered because I wasn't happy. Previously I would come home all bubbly, either because I'd sold a policy or because I'd dug up a contact that I had high hopes for.

Now I was down all the time. But I kept trying to remember that that is work and this is home, and I tried to keep the two separate. But in the middle of this bad spell, I was very down in the mouth.

However, having been successful in the past, I knew that I wasn't doing anything vastly different now. Sure, as the saga of no sales continued, I became defeatist, but then I remembered a piece of advice someone had once given me: 'You've got to welcome that "No" because you are now one step closer to that "Yes".' I came to think that, having received all these 'No's', sooner or later I was going to be getting a load of 'Yeses'! And that ended up being true.

Then I found that my managers were having no better luck than I was. This was like a problem shared – if someone else isn't having any more success than you, then you ask yourself, 'Is it all my fault, or is it the fault of the situation I've found myself in?'

Actually it was a suggestion from my wife that helped me turn the corner. She said, 'If what you're doing now isn't working, why don't you try something completely different?'

One of the things that, in the past, I had been quite successful at was 'cold calling'. I'd left that behind when I started building a business out of renewals and following referrals. But now, with that having fallen to the wayside and with nothing to lose, I thought I'd give cold calling a try. I did a leaflet drop and then followed it up with visits. The first bit of business I finally did was tiny but to me, at that time, it felt like it was worth a fortune! The corner had finally been turned.

Eventually, because I'd been continuing with my other work, results started to come through, and in December I realized that I had had my most successful year ever.

Mike's difficult experience is certainly a common one in selling. Most sales people have experienced at least one 'blank' period. But some are unable to turn the negative situation around – for them, it's the beginning of a downward spiral that affects their confidence and work behaviour, impacting on their earnings and often ending with them giving up and leaving the job.

So how was it that Mike was able to become successful again? It wasn't due to a change in external circumstances – the large company with whom he did business was on the verge of closing and many of Mike's clients (both existing and potential) were made redundant. Nothing had changed there. It could be argued that it was just luck that Mike became top adviser in the office again. Possibly. However, I would suggest that it was something else – Mike's attitude. Sure, his successful attitude faltered during his bad patch. He started to question his own ability, and his confidence fell. This affected his work (he stopped doing the administration part of his work, essential to the smooth functioning of his sales job, and he started to give up and go home early), and so a downward spiral began to develop.

But Mike was able to overturn the downward spiral by changing the way he viewed the situation. He began to see it as a temporary setback rather than a personal failure. This, in turn, impacted on his behaviour – he started to open his mind to new ideas and he changed the way he went about his job. The change in attitude and behaviour enabled him to persevere until he reached his goal.

What Mike had was the *psychological resilience* to get through the difficult times, and he also had *initiative* – two essential factors for success in selling.

Resilience + Initiative

↓

Peak sales performance

To be a successful salesperson, you need to be enterprising and to have 'get up and go'. In other words, you need to be a self-starter, proactive, entrepreneurial. Take a look at a sales person whom you regard as being highly successful (maybe it's you!). You'll see these characteristics very clearly. But initiative is only part of the formula for peak sales performance. Difficulties and setbacks are an intrinsic part of selling, so successful salespeople must also have the ability to bounce back, to persevere, to turn obstacles into opportunities.

But what enables a salesperson to be persistent and use initiative under high pressure?

Research in psychology indicates that the way we interpret our successes and failures determines how resilient and proactive we are.

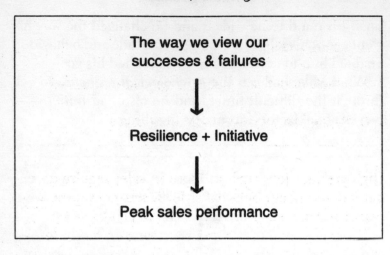

Some people have trouble believing this fact. They claim that, as long as they have one success, they'll go on and have more. It may seem like this, but we now know from years of research that this is not exactly correct. Sure, having a success helps. But how you *interpret* your success (or failure) has a greater impact on whether you'll be successful in the future.

Your *attributional style*

The way people explain the events that happen to them is known as their 'attributional style'. Each of us has our own particular attributional style. For example, some people usually blame others for their failures, while others tend to blame themselves. Some give general reasons for their successes, while others give reasons specific to each situation. Each person's complex pattern of explanations determines that individual's levels of resilience and initiative. In turn, these factors reveal that person's likelihood of success or failure.

A. Success/failure

B. Beliefs about why the success/failure occurred

C. Resilience, initiative, high productivity

High-pressure jobs such as those in sales require an extremely strong attributional style. It separates those who persist and succeed from those who fail and give up.

There is a good deal of evidence for this. For instance, one research study of the US financial services industry[1] showed that sales agents with a strong attributional style – that is, those who scored in the top 10% – sold 88% more insurance in their first two years than those who scored in the bottom 10%. Another study, this time in the UK,[2] showed similar results: not only did agents with a positive attributional style sell significantly more policies, these policies were of a higher value than those sold by agents with a weaker attributional style. In the retail sector,[3] sales assistants with a helpful attributional style have been proven to be more customer-focused and more proactive in achieving sales than their colleagues with a less helpful attributional style. With retail managers,[4] a positive attributional style has been shown to be indirectly related to their career success, personal strength and customer focus.

[1] Seligman & Schulman (1986), *Journal of Personality and Social Psychology*, 50: 4, 832–8.

[2] Corr & Gray (1996), *Journal of Occupational and Organisational Psychology*, 69: 83–7.

[3] Patterson & Silvester (1998), *People Management*, April: 46–8.

[4] Flint-Taylor, J. (1998), Doctoral Thesis, University of London.

The evidence is unequivocal: *a strong attributional style is a critical factor in sales success*. And the good news is that it can be learned.

Just like with your core beliefs, the first step is to become aware of your attributional style. Then you check to see if it is helpful – that is, whether it is enhancing your success. Then, if it's not helpful, you substitute more effective ways of thinking; and finally, you practise the new ways of thinking until they become habits.

The four steps to enhancing success

1 Recognize your attributional style.
2 Determine whether it is helpful.
3 If unhelpful, substitute more effective ways of thinking.
4 Practise the new ways of thinking until they become habits.

By becoming aware of and managing your own attributional style, you can take control of your success. So, let's get started on the first step: recognizing your attributional style.

The question 'Why?'

After we have had a success or setback, we look for a reason for the outcome – in other words, *why* it occurred. For example, 'The customer bought the car because I helped her choose one that suited her needs' or 'I'll exceed my target this month because I've made a couple of really big sales.' We may not be aware of looking for reasons for the good and bad outcomes that occur, but we do it quite frequently, as often as once a minute, particularly after important or unexpected outcomes. Only a small part of the reason that we choose is determined by the actual situation; predominantly, the explanation we come up with is determined by our attributional style.

The three parts of attributional style

The attributional style of each of us is made up of three sets of beliefs. Beliefs are the crux of the programme contained in this book. They are the Bs in the ABC model. I've outlined the three sets of attributional beliefs below.* Look at each one in turn and then apply them to your own situation.

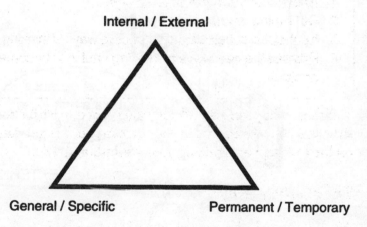

Internal / External

General / Specific   Permanent / Temporary

Internal/external beliefs

Some of our beliefs are *internal* – that is, 'I caused the event; it was due to me.' Other beliefs are *external* – 'Other people or circumstances caused the event – not me.'

---

* Adapted from Optimism ABC by Dr M. E. P. Seligman & Foresight Inc.

Take a look at the tennis players in the illustration. The winner's belief is *internal*: he believes that his success is due to him. The loser's belief is *external*: he puts his defeat down to his opponent's fine playing.

Now let's apply the same internal/external idea to selling. Imagine that you have greatly exceeded your sales target this month.

What would be an internal reason for this success? Write this down below.

_____

_____

_____

What would be an external reason? Write this down, too.

_____

_____

_____

Now check your answers. An example of an internal reason for exceeding a sales target would be 'my good selling skills'. An example of an external reason would be 'my manager's help'.

To be very successful in selling, you have to learn to take credit for your successes. Looking for internal reasons for successes helps to boost self-esteem and achievement. *But the reasons must be realistic* – otherwise they're just examples of empty 'positive thinking', which has no value at all. As far as bad outcomes are concerned, it doesn't matter whether they are due to internal or external factors; as long as you don't take them too personally, they will not undermine your future success.

Permanent/temporary beliefs

Another way of explaining good and bad outcomes is to view them as either permanent or temporary.

A *permanent* cause is a long-lasting one, something that will always happen or will happen again in the future – for example, 'I'll always be like this.' A *temporary* cause, on the other hand, is transient in nature – for instance, 'This is just a short-term setback.'

Take a look at the tennis players below. The winner's belief is permanent: he is attributing his victory to the consistency of his fine playing. The loser's explanation is temporary: he's having a bad today, but the implication is that tomorrow might be different.

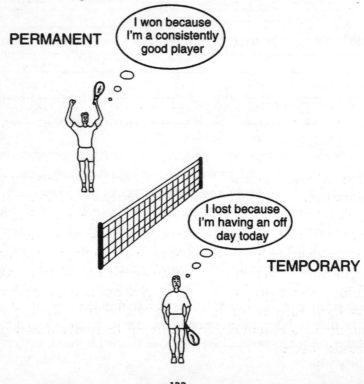

Now let's apply the permanent/temporary dimension to sales.

What would be a permanent reason for having exceeded your target?

_____

_____

_____

What would be a temporary reason?

_____

_____

_____

OK, now check your answers. An example of a permanent reason for exceeding the sales target is 'I plan well.' An example of a temporary reason would be 'I had a good month this month.'

You've seen the difference between permanent and temporary reasons, so why are they important for success in selling? Well, we know that salespeople who habitually put their successes down to temporary reasons – such as 'I was lucky' or 'I happened to be at the right place at the right time' – do nothing to build up their confidence for future sales. And those who also give permanent reasons for their failures (such as 'I'll never be able to sell this product') are actually *undermining* their likelihood of future success.

Looking for permanent reasons for good outcomes and temporary reasons for bad outcomes is the way to enhance success in selling.

General/specific beliefs

The third part of attributional style is whether we view the reasons for good and bad outcomes as general (that is, affecting many different circumstances) or specific (limited to an isolated event or a specific situation).

Take a look at the tennis players opposite. The winner's belief is general: he puts his success down to his ability to play on *all* types of court. The loser, by contrast, is putting his defeat down to one specific aspect of his game: his volleying.

Now let's again turn to the example of having exceeded your target.

What would be a general reason for this happening? Write this down below.

_____

_____

_____

What would be a specific reason for this? Write this down.

_____

_____

_____

OK, so now let's check your answers again. An example of a general reason for exceeding the target would be 'I can

spot good sales opportunities.' An example of a specific reason would be 'I closed a particularly big sale.'

Giving general reasons for good outcomes enhances success in many different areas of selling – *and* in other areas of your life, too – so it's important to look for them when you've had a good result, remembering that, of course, they must be realistic. However, identifying a general reason for setbacks and problems is destructive – it leaves you open to applying this negative reason to other areas of your job or life.

Beliefs that undermine

Take a closer look at the three sets of tennis cartoons in this section, which illustrate the three types of beliefs. Each illustrates a beneficial way of thinking about an outcome. In the first cartoon, the winner gives an internal reason for his success, while the unsuccessful tennis player attributes an external cause for his loss. In the second cartoon, the winner states a permanent reason for his positive outcome, while the loser gives a temporary one for his result. In other words, the winning player in both cartoons believes that he brought about the positive outcome and that this is a lasting quality in himself. At the same time, the losing player doesn't blame himself and he believes that his defeat is only temporary.

Furthermore, in the third cartoon, the winner gives a general statement for his achievement and the loser makes a specific one about his failure. Both are beneficial choices. By focusing on a general aspect of his game, the winner's thinking acts like pebble dropped into a pool, with positive ripples extending outward into other aspects of his tennis playing. It will boost his confidence and success in other games on any type of court. By focusing on a specific cause, the loser has isolated the reason for his loss to just his volleying in that game.

But what if the winner had explained his success as '*I won because my opponent played badly today*.' This is an *external* explanation (he's attributing his victory to his opponent, not himself); it's *specific*, relating only to that particular opponent; and it's *temporary* – the next opponent might play better. This way of thinking about achievements does nothing to enhance the likelihood of winning in the future. In fact, it actually undermines success.

Yet society expects us to explain our successes in just this way – external, temporary and specific. It is the 'modest' way to think. But such a thinking pattern minimizes successes and reduces self-esteem because the successes are not being added to our view of ourselves – they are being given away.

So rather than thinking 'I won because my opponent played badly today' (specific, external, temporary), the winner of the tennis match would do better to think 'I won because I'm a strong tennis player' (permanent, internal, general).

Beliefs that enhance success

We plan and work for the majority of good outcomes that occur in our lives. It is important, therefore, that we recognize them and take credit for what we are due.

To enhance your success in selling, therefore, you need to look for Permanent, Internal and General – PIG – reasons for your good outcomes. This means that you look for a role that you've played to bring about the positive event (even if it's only a small role). At the same time, it needs to be something about you that you can do regularly and in many different areas of your work or life.

PIG reasons for good outcomes are the secret of success. You don't have to walk around blowing your own trumpet, but you do have to *think* in this way if you want to achieve excellence in selling.

And what about the tennis player who lost the match? What if he had explained his loss as 'I'm hopeless at sport.' This is an *internal* reason for his defeat. That's OK, because some of our problems are due to something about ourselves. But where the loser gets into trouble is that his reason is also *permanent* (it implies that he's hopelcss now and will be in future, too) and it's *general* (involving all sport, not just this game of tennis). This type of thinking will undermine his motivation, confidence and hope for future games. He may as well give up now – and he probably will!

To enhance his future tennis playing, the loser needs to view his defeat as a *specific* and *temporary* setback. This implies that he'll change his strategy next time or ask for advice on how to improve his game in order to maximize his chances of a win next time. And most importantly, it will not reduce his motivation and confidence – on the contrary, he will probably feel even more determined.

Can you see the relevance of this for selling? Individuals who claim that, as long as they have one success, they'll go on and have more are failing to recognize the impact of their thinking. How you interpret successes (and failures) has a greater impact on your initiative and resilience – and, therefore, your future success – than the actual presence or absence of a success. You can enhance your personal performance by ensuring that you think about good and bad outcomes in a successful way.

The formula for successful thinking is:

For positive outcomes:
PIG beliefs: permanent, internal, general

For negative outcomes:
STI/E beliefs: specific, temporary,
internal or external

This is the winning formula.

Of the 3 parts of your attributional style, the two most important in the psychology of successful selling are the general/specific and the permanent/temporary. As for the internal/external dimension, its impact is greatest on your self-esteem.

As long as bad outcomes are seen as being due to specific and temporary factors, either way of thinking – STI or STE – is effective in the psychology of success. Even if the bad outcome is caused by you, it is not due to something enduring about you and therefore a change of strategy can change the outcome. Whereas a PIG belief for a bad outcome – in which the outcome is caused by you because of something negative about you that is long-lasting and affects everything you do – will often be so overwhelming that you will be at a loss to come up with anything to overcome it.

Look back at the case study about Mike (page 111). Do you now notice that the point at which he started to view his 'blank patch' as a temporary setback (STE) rather than a personal failure (PIG) was the moment when he began to overturn the downward spiral? His change in attitude

Beliefs that enhance success		Beliefs that undermine success	
A. Success	A. Setback	A. Success	A. Setback
B. Permanent Internal Global	B. Specific Temporary Internal/External	B. Specific External Temporary	B. Permanent Internal Global
C. Motivation Confidence Success	C. Motivation Confidence Success	C. Demotivation Frustration Decreased productivity	C. Demotivation Frustration Decreased productivity

then impacted on his behaviour – he started to open his mind to new ideas and he modified the way he went about his job. The change in attitude and behaviour enabled him to achieve even greater success than he had previously.

Explaining the causes of successes and failures

Consider this example. Sally, a city trader loses an important sale. She thinks: 'I never get anything right.'

Below, break this thought down into the three parts of attributional style. Circle whether it is internal or external, permanent or temporary, general or specific. Then in the light of its attributional parts write in the likely consequence of the thought in terms of Sally's feelings and behaviour.

Event: Loss of an important sale

Thought: 'I never get anything right'

     Internal or External

     Permanent or Temporary

     General or Specific

Likely consequence: _____

OK, lets check your answers. The explanation 'I never get anything right' is internal because Sally attributes the failure to her incompetence.

It is also a *permanent* explanation because it relates to an unchanging or constant feature of her functioning – namely, her uselessness. And it is *general* because it refers to a wide range of situations – for instance, she might also use this explanation to explain why she burned the supper or played a bad game of golf.

Such a thinking pattern, if widely applied, would tend to magnify all failures and lead to feelings of hopelessness and depression, especially if the event was an important one. People who make permanent, internal and global – PIG – explanations for bad events are more likely to give up when adversity hits. Research has shown that they are also more apt to become depressed and to get sick, and less likely to live up to their potential. In light of this, it is very important for you to identify the kinds of explanations that you give yourself for bad events and to learn to replace unproductive thoughts with productive, powerful ones.

Now imagine that Sally had actually closed the same sale and attributed it to the fact that the customers were particularly easy.

Below, break this thought down into its three attributional parts and then think about its likely effect on Sally's feelings and behaviour.

Event: Closed an important sale

Thought: 'The customers were easy'

       Internal or External

       Permanent or Temporary

       General or Specific

Likely consequence: _____

Such an explanation is *external* because it relates success to a characteristic of the customers, rather than to the individual salesperson. It is *temporary* because easy customers cannot be relied upon in all sales transactions. And it is *specific* because it cannot be used to explain success in any other setting.

If you *consistently* believe that the causes of your successes are due to external, specific and temporary factors such as good luck or an easy sale, you are at risk of low motivation, low self-belief and not achieving your potential.

Examining your own successes

Now take a look at the success you wrote down on page 106 in the previous stage. To what did you first attribute it? Please tick your answer below.

Your ability?	☐
Luck?	☐
The effort you had put in?	☐
The ease of the task?	☐
Positive circumstances?	☐

Each of the five reasons above can be broken down into the three attributional parts: Internal/External, Permanent/Temporary, General/Specific. See if you can do this. The answers are at the end of this chapter (page 141).

Now look at the main reason for your success that you wrote down *after* you had been interviewed about it. Break it into its three attributional parts.

Reason: _____

- Permanent/Temporary
- Internal/External
- General/Specific

Can you now see why I suggested that your interviewer should write down all the skills and abilities underpinning your success? It is because I was leading you towards PIG reasons for your success. Can you remember how the PIG reasons felt at the time you were being interviewed?

Now ask yourself: Do you generally tend to give permanent, internal and general (PIG) reasons for your successes? Yes/No *(please circle)*

Turn to the Success Diary that you wrote during the past week. Look at the causes you gave for your successes and break them into the three attributional parts. Were they mainly PIG causes?

Be warned: For a reason to be a 'real' PIG, it must be written in the present tense – e.g. 'I plan well' – not in the past tense: 'I planned well.' The latter would be temporary, referring only to that occasion, not permanent. This is very important in the psychology of success.

If any of the reasons you wrote down were not PIGs, please change them now. Remember to look for a part that you've played – even just a small one – in each success, so that you can do it again in many different areas. I'm not suggesting that you should be immodest. Rather, it is important that you acknowledge to yourself the specific roles you have played in your successes.

Looking at your failures and setbacks

Now let's turn to failures and setbacks. We all have them,

but do you look for specific and temporary causes (STI/E) for yours? Yes/No *(please circle)*

It may seem rather awkward initially. But remember, you don't have to tell other people; as long as you're thinking this way, you will be enhancing your success.

At first, you need to learn to do it consciously, but with practice, it will become a habit. The trick is to have some of these thoughts up your sleeve for when you have a setback. (The same is true for PIG thoughts when you have successes.) This is what I suggest you do in the box below.

Beliefs that lead to success

Think of five PIG reasons for positive outcomes and five STI/E reasons for negative outcomes that are relevant for you. I'll give you a couple of examples of each. Write yours in the box below and use them when you have a good or bad outcome. These are the beliefs that lead to success.

A. Good outcome	A. Bad outcome
B. Examples of PIG beliefs: 'I'm a good communicator' 'I'm organized' _____ _____ _____ _____ _____	**B. Examples of STI/E beliefs:** 'I went about it the wrong way' 'The conditions weren't right this time' _____ _____ _____ _____
C. Results Resilience Initiative Success	**C. Results** Resilience Initiative Success

Testing your beliefs

We have examined how certain types of beliefs about the causes of successes and failures are associated with increased resilience, initiative and further success, while other types result in a sapping of motivation, increased frustration and a drop in success. Finally, let's test these beliefs in your job.

Think of a recent situation involving a negative outcome and another one with a positive result, and write these in the box opposite. Then come up with a STI/E reason (i.e. a helpful one) for the negative outcome and a PIG (unhelpful) reason for it. Describe the impact that each of the different views would have on your mood and behaviour and rate the feelings and behaviour out of 10. Similarly, come up with both a helpful (PIG) and an unhelpful (STI/E) reason for the positive outcome, and describe and rate the resulting mood and behaviour that would accompany each explanation.

Now compare the helpful and unhelpful versions. Can you feel the difference?

Conclusion

In Stage 6, you have learned some very powerful thinking strategies to enhance your success. These techniques will assist you to feel empowered in your job and in life in general, to have more control over the ups and downs, to be more motivated, resilient and successful. But just like learning any new skill, such as driving a car, you need to *practise* your new techniques.

Types of beliefs: personal work examples

Situation (A)	Thoughts/beliefs (B)	Outcome (C) (feelings/ behaviour) (rate 1–10)
Write down a work situation that had a negative outcome for you.	1 A helpful reason for the negative outcome (STI/E) 2 An unhelpful reason for the negative outcome (PIG)	1 2
Write down a work situation that had a positive outcome for you.	1 A helpful reason for the positive outcome (PIG) 2 An unhelpful reason for the positive outcome (STI/E)	1 2

Next week's tasks

1 Carry out the activities that you have planned for this coming week. After each one, make a note on the Thought Audit opposite of the result of the event and the cause of the result. Rate your causes as either Internal or External, Permanent or Temporary and General or Specific.

The purpose of this activity is for you to make positive but realistic attributions about your successes and difficulties – to take credit for the positive events for which you are responsible, and not give your successes away or minimize them. Therefore please do not make up causes, but look closely for ones that you may normally have missed. Ask yourself if you are enhancing your self-belief and future success or are you unwittingly reducing them by thinking in an unhelpful way.

Thoughts Audit

Week beginning ....../........../.......

Event	Outcome	Cause of the outcome	Rating Internal/ External Permanent/ Temporary Global/ Specific

2 Plan the coming week using the plan below, making sure that there is a good balance of activities (including rewards for good outcomes).

Weekly Plan
Week beginning ...... / ...... / ......

	......day	......day	......day	......day	......day	......day	......day
AM							
PM							
Evening							

140

3 Complete the sixth week's entry in your Personal Log (page 161): 'Something I have learned (about myself, my job, etc.) which I will find useful.'

Answers to the exercise on page 133

Your ability = Permanent, Internal, General (PIG)

Luck = Specific, Temporary, External (STE)

The effort you had put in = Specific, Temporary, Internal (STI)

The ease of the task = Specific, Temporary, External (STE)

Positive circumstances = Specific, Temporary, External (STE)

Stage 7:

Planning and Action for Success

You've learned some powerful techniques to train your mind to achieve higher levels of performance. It's an 'inside out' approach to success – working from your thinking to your feelings and behaviour and then to your results. In this last stage, we're going to look at some different ways of applying these techniques and undertake some action planning for the future. But first, let's see how you're getting on with your thinking.

During the past week, you analysed the attributions you made for positive and negative events that occurred in your job. Did you find that you viewed your successes and failures in a helpful way? Revisit the Thoughts Audit you completed during the week. Look at the causes you wrote for your successes and failures, and how you rated those causes. If any of the causes were unhelpful – that is, not PIG reasons for successes, and not STI/E reasons for negative outcomes – use the Four Challenging Questions below to develop more helpful ways of viewing the outcomes.

- Am I making any **thinking errors**?

- Where is the **evidence** that this was the cause of my success/failure?

- What is an **alternative** way of viewing it?
- What **action** can I take for the future?

It's important to keep practising these cognitive techniques. Knowing that you have the strengths and strategies to bring about success and reduce the impact of setbacks is a valuable asset to have.

Distraction techniques

There may be times when it is unhelpful to focus on your thinking. When you are concentrating on an important task or when you are trying to get to sleep, it makes more sense to clear your mind. This doesn't mean that it won't be useful to return to those thoughts later. It's just not useful to focus on them right at that time.

Can you think of any other situations when it would be counter-productive to focus on your thoughts? Write them below.

_____

_____

_____

_____

_____

Whenever you find yourself in a situation in which you do not want to stop and examine your thoughts, but wish instead to break their current hold on you, there are some *distraction techniques* that you might find useful:

Focus your attention on your breathing

Take slow regular breaths in and out. Some people find it helpful to breathe in to the count of 4 and out for 5. Your stomach should rise as you breathe in and fall as you push the air out of your lungs. Do this for 3–4 minutes to feel the full effect. Not only will it help you take your attention off troublesome thoughts, it will also calm you down if you're feeling upset.

Write down the troublesome thoughts

In other words, try to offload them on to a piece of paper when they occur. This assures you that the issue is not being forgotten or neglected, and helps you to return to it later. For some people, this will only work if combined with the next technique.

Set aside a specific time for thinking things over

This might be 30 minutes in the morning or any time that fits in with your daily schedule and when you are usually relaxed. The only time to avoid thinking things over is right before you go to bed at night, because focusing on possibly contentious thoughts will make it difficult for you to fall asleep.

Limit yourself to thinking things through only at your scheduled time. If you find yourself thinking about things at other times, write down your thoughts to put them out of your mind until your 'thinking time' comes around.

Thought breaking

If you haven't time to deal with a particular set of thoughts, do something that breaks the continuity of those thoughts.

You may need to experiment to find the right kind of activity. Here are some examples:

- break off and make yourself a drink;

- switch to a different task;

- talk to someone who is unconnected with the issue about a totally unrelated subject;

- take a shower;

- do some physical activity, such as going for a walk, gardening, playing a game or participating in sport;

- read something amusing or cheerful;

- do a crossword puzzle;

- listen to a piece of music that takes you out of yourself.

Sometimes it only takes five minutes for the unhelpful thought pattern to be broken. But don't forget to return to the thoughts later to challenge them.

Try out each of the distraction techniques during the next week to discover the one that suits you best. You might find that a combination of two, three or all four is the most effective.

Applying the strategies to other areas

Thus far, we've focused on the use of the cognitive-behavioral techniques on your thinking and behaviour in your job. However, the same techniques can be used just as effectively in other areas, such as at home and with your clients.

'Bringing it all back home'

A career in sales can be very demanding. The sales targets to meet on a weekly basis, the accounts system, the long hours, the calls at home – these can all carry over to affect the way you feel in your private life. You may find yourself becoming irritable or wanting to isolate yourself from your family. Your mood may also affect that of your partner and children.

If you notice this happening, it can be useful to analyse and challenge your thoughts by completing a Thought Record. You may also wish to use the 'downward arrow' technique (page 97), asking yourself, 'What does that mean to me?' to uncover some of the deeper thoughts that may be affecting your mood.

You can also help your partner and/or children understand some of *their* feelings by guiding them through a Thought Record. For example, your family may misinterpret your long hours or your preoccupation with work as reflecting a change in your feelings towards them. You can use the evidence, alternatives and action questions to help them understand the situation and their interpretation of it. At the very least, this will open the lines of communication and could help to alleviate unnecessary fears.

In addition, you can use these techniques to help your family deal with issues in their own lives that are unrelated to your career. Not only will you be teaching them valuable skills, but it would also consolidate your understanding of the concepts and techniques that you have learned from this book.

Start off by teaching them the basic ABC model (page 6), emphasizing the link between what we believe and how we feel and behave. Tell them about the common thinking errors and then teach them the Four Challenging Questions (page 64), focusing on how to gather evidence and generate alternatives. You could also share with them your dreams and goals, and help them to set goals for them-selves. And don't forget to teach them to think PIG thoughts – these are just as important for your loved ones as they are for you.

By using these techniques together, they will become valuable tools in your family's armoury, helping all of you to problem-solve and deal with each other fairly and effec-tively.

Dealing with clients' thoughts

The same procedures that are helpful in dealing with your own thoughts and feelings can also be used with your clients.

Handling client concerns and objections is a key skill in selling. You will have developed your own effective tech-niques for doing this. The strategies in this book provide an additional approach.

First, use the ABC model (page 6) to understand the client's reaction. Try to elicit as many of your client's thoughts as possible. Ask questions like:

- 'How does that seem to you?'
- 'Can you tell me a little more?'
- 'What is going through your mind?'
- 'I'm not sure what you're thinking.'

Try to use open questions that encourage the client to tell you his/her thoughts, rather than closed questions that are likely to result in one-word answers such as 'yes' or

Dealing with clients' thoughts

A. Situation	B. Clients' thoughts or words	C. Outcome	D. Your challenge	E. New outcome

'no'. (Save the closed questions for the final stage of the sales process, when a single word – 'yes' – is all required of the client!)

From the client's thoughts, you can predict the likely outcome. For example, say as a result of your skilful questioning, the client articulates the following thoughts 'Well actually we've tried this before and it didn't suit us'. If you didn't deal with this objection, the likely outcome, of course, would be no sale.

So you use the Four Challenging Questions to respond to the client's objections or concerns:

1. *Is s/he making any thinking errors?*
   First, be aware of any thinking errors your client is making. Just make a mental note of any you identify (rather than informing the client!), in order to help you to formulate your responses. For example, is the client jumping to conclusions? In this case, you might wish to think of facts you could supply to fill in evidence the client seems to be missing. Is the client thinking in black and white terms? You might offer some alternative views, perhaps from other clients. Is the client magnifying? In this case, you might think of some action that could be taken to challenge these thoughts.

2. *What is the evidence?*
   Show your client the evidence or the facts. The best way to do this is through questioning, rather than telling. For example, in the situation above, a good strategy would be to focus on the word 'suit', and find out what the client perceives as suiting their needs. Then present some evidence to show the client how the product or service you're offering does suit their needs.

3. *What is an alternative way of viewing the situation?*
   Here you present the client with some other possibilities. Effective questions to ask include:
   • Is there another way of looking at this?
   • Are there other possibilities?
   • Maybe we could …

4. *What action can I/we take?*
   And lastly, you explore the next steps with the client.
   • Where do we go next?
   • What would you like me to do?

In the example mentioned above, for instance, you might offer to collect feedback from other clients, or refer the client to similar clients who found your product suited their needs (evidence).

The Four Challenging Questions represent the D in the ABCDE model. Not only are they useful tools for enhancing your own thinking, they are effective strategies for challenging client objections and concerns. The new outcome, E, will be greater selling success.

The ABCDE model offers an additional set of strategies to those you may already use for understanding your client reactions and responding to their objections or concerns.

Why don't you try using them in this way on the Thought Record on page 148? Think of a current situation, preferably a sale that you still haven't managed to close, and write it in the A column on the Thought Record. In the B column, write down your client's thoughts. Include those that your client has actually articulated to you and those you have ascertained from his/her questions, body language and behaviour. In the C column, wrote down the outcome to date (e.g. no sale).

Now in the D column, evaluate and challenge your client's thoughts using the Four Challenging Questions:

- Is the client making any thinking errors?
- What is the evidence?
- Are there other ways of viewing the situation?
- What action can I/we take?

Once you have gone through this process on the Thought Record, the next step is for you to contact your client, in order to achieve a new outcome E.

From the client's thoughts, you can predict the likely outcome.

So, you use the Four Challenging Questions (page 64) to respond to the client's objections or concerns. In the situation above, you could focus on the word 'suit' and use the evidence question to show the client how the product or service you are offering may well suit them. Or you could also show the client an alternative way of viewing the situation.

Review

That brings us to the end of this programme. By completing all the stages of *Successful Selling*, you have learnt a number of strategies that will enhance your sales effectiveness. Here's a list of what we've covered.

- ABC model (page 6)
- Automatic thoughts (page 11)
- Thought catching (page 12)
- High-performance goal setting (page 18)
- Personal motivating activities (page 27)

- Managing time creatively (page 31)
- Planning (page 32)
- Task breakdown techniques (page 34)
- Self-rewards (page 37)
- Thought recording (page 44)
- Stress-producing and stress-reducing thoughts (page 49)
- Common thinking errors (page 53)
- Four Challenging Questions (page 64)
- Core beliefs (page 88)
- Attributional style (page 116)
- PIG thinking (page 127)
- Distraction techniques (page 143)
- Using the strategies at home and with your clients (page 146)

Through my research, I've been able to demonstrate that sales people who use these techniques have greater job satisfaction, self-esteem, motivation and psychological well-being, they stay in their jobs longer and they achieve higher sales success. But the techniques must be continually practised to be effective. To help you to do this, I suggest you complete a plan of action.

A *plan of action*

In your Personal Log (page 161), you have made notes of points that were of particular relevance to you. Look through these now and at any other notes that you may have made. Then choose two areas that you would like to work on further. These become your goals.

Write your two goals on the top of the Action Plan on page 155. Possible goals might include:

- Keeping a daily diary of successes and setbacks for six weeks. Try to discover any realistic possible causes that you normally miss (don't make up any) and look for evidence for each. Try to enhance your thinking by learning to re-evaluate everyday situations.

- Implementing a time-management system.

- Doing some more reading on this subject on a regular basis (see page 165).

- Planning to do ten cold canvasses every week.

- Completing a Prospect Register and aiming to have 30 hot prospects at any one time.

- Planning to do a predetermined number of sales presentations per week.

Now check your goals to make sure they are positive, realistic and measurable.

Next, break each goal into small achievable steps, allocate time for each step, and intersperse realistic rewards. The first step should be achievable within the next three weeks.

Blocks

When you pursue a goal, particularly if you aim to implement new strategies such as the ones you have learned from this book, you will undoubtedly encounter obstacles and setbacks. It is important to try to trouble-shoot possible problems, or blocks, in advance. This can be done by anticipating the situations in which setbacks are likely.

What are some possible obstacles that you might face when trying to implement your goals? What setbacks might you encounter? Common obstacles/blocks that might prevent you from achieving your goals include:

- being too busy;
- negative attitudes (your own or other people's) towards self-improvement;
- setting unrealistic goals;
- not seeing a problem as your own;
- being too stressed;
- expecting others to achieve the goal for you.

On your Action Plan, jot down any obstacles that you think might block you from achieving your goals.

What are some possible methods that could be used for overcoming the obstacles? What additional skills are needed?

Add to your Action Plan any strategies that you can think of that will help you to beat any obstacles you might encounter on the way to achieving your goals.

Conclusion

At the end of a book like this, it is customary to wish the reader good luck. But I'm not going to do that. Of course, I wish you lots of success in your career. But with the techniques you've learned, it's not a question of luck, but rather of good thinking and lots of practice!

Action Plan

Goal 1

Steps	Time	Rewards	Possible blocks	Beating the blocks

Action Plan

Goal 2

Steps	Time	Rewards	Possible blocks	Beating the blocks

Tasks for the coming weeks

1 To ensure that the benefits you have gained from completing the *Successful Selling* programme persist and that you are maintaining the ways of successful thinking and acting that you have learned, you should complete a Thoughts Audit every week for the next six weeks (additional blank copies are provided in the Appendix). After that time, you may no longer need to put your thoughts on paper – you'll be able to check and modify them in your head.

2 If you find that something is bothering you, you should complete a Thought Record (additional blank copies are provided in the Appendix). Tap into your thoughts and, if necessary, use the 'downward arrow' technique (page 97) to uncover any deep beliefs, particularly if your feelings are unusually strong. Then challenge the thoughts that are producing the unwanted feelings.

3 Complete the seventh week's entry in your Personal Log (page 161): 'Something I have learned (about myself, my job, etc.) which I will find useful.'

Thoughts Audit

Week beginning ...../........./.......

Event	Outcome	Cause of the outcome	Rating Internal/External Perm/Temp Global/Specific

Thought Record

A. Situation	B. Thoughts (rate 0–10)	C. Feelings (rate 0–10)	D. Evaluate and challenge unhelpful thoughts	E. New feelings (rate 0–10)
			Thinking errors *Evidence* *Alternatives* *Action*	

Personal Log

Something new I have learned (about myself, my job, etc) which I will find useful:

Week 1 ....

....

....

....

....

....

....

....

....

....

Something new I have learned (about myself, my job, etc) which I will find useful:

Week 2...

....

....

....

....

....

....

....

....

Week 3 ....

....

....

....

....

....

....

....

....

Something new I have learned (about myself, my job, etc) which I will find useful:

Week 4 ....

....

....

....

....

....

....

....

....

....

Week 5 ....

....

....

....

....

....

....

....

....

....

Something new I have learned (about myself, my job, etc) which I will find useful:

Week 6 ....

....

....

....

....

....

....

....

....

Week 7 ....

....

....

....

....

....

....

....

....

Further Reading

Burns, D. (1990) *The Feeling Good Handbook*. Penguin Books, New York.

Conger, J. (1998) 'The Art of Persuasion'. *Harvard Business Review*.

Seligman, M. (1991) *Learned Optimism*. Alfred A. Knopf, New York.

Whitmore, J. (1996) *Coaching for Performance* (2nd ed.). Nicholas Brearly Publishing, London.

Index

Appendix

Catching thoughts

Date	Positive thoughts	Tally	Negative thoughts	Tally

Catching thoughts

Date	Positive thoughts	Tally	Negative thoughts	Tally

Catching thoughts

Date	Positive thoughts	Tally	Negative thoughts	Tally

Weekly Plan

Week beginning ..../......./.......

	.....day	.....day	.....day	.....day	.....day	.....day	.....day
AM							
PM							
Evening							

Weekly Plan

Week beginning ...../...../.....

	......day	......day	......day	......day	......day	......day	......day
AM							
PM							
Evening							

Weekly Plan

Week beginning ....../....../......

	......day	......day	......day	......day	......day	......day	......day
AM							
PM							
Evening							

Prospecting Register

Client/ Prospect	Current Business	Canvass Details	Outcome	Cause of the Outcome

Prospecting Register

Client/ Prospect	Current Business	Canvass Details	Outcome	Cause of the Outcome

Prospecting Register

Client/ Prospect	Current Business	Canvass Details	Outcome	Cause of the Outcome

Thoughts Audit

Week beginning ....../......../.......

Event	Outcome	Cause of the outcome	Rating Internal/External Perm/Temp Global/Specific

Thoughts Audit

Week beginning ...../........./.......

Event	Outcome	Cause of the outcome	Rating Internal/External Perm/Temp Global/Specific

Thoughts Audit

Week beginning ....../......../.......

Event	Outcome	Cause of the outcome	Rating Internal/External Perm/Temp Global/Specific

Appendix

Thoughts Audit

Week beginning ...../........./.......

Event	Outcome	Cause of the outcome	Rating Internal/External Perm/Temp Global/Specific

Thoughts Audit

Week beginning ....../........./.......

Event	Outcome	Cause of the outcome	Rating Internal/External Perm/Temp Global/Specific

Thoughts Audit

Week beginning ....../........./.......

Event	Outcome	Cause of the outcome	Rating Internal/External Perm/Temp Global/Specific

Thought Record

A. Situation	B. Thoughts (rate 0–10)	C. Feelings (rate 0–10)	D. Evaluate and challenge unhelpful thoughts	E. New feelings (rate 0–10)
			Thinking errors	
			Evidence	
			Alternatives	
			Action	

Thought Record

A. Situation	B. Thoughts (rate 0–10)	C. Feelings (rate 0–10)	D. Evaluate and challenge unhelpful thoughts	E. New feelings (rate 0–10)
			Thinking errors	
			Evidence	
			Alternatives	
			Action	

Thought Record

A. Situation	B. Thoughts (rate 0–10)	C. Feelings (rate 0–10)	D. Evaluate and challenge unhelpful thoughts	E. New feelings (rate 0–10)
			Thinking errors	
			Evidence	
			Alternatives	
			Action	

Thought Record

A. Situation	B. Thoughts (rate 0–10)	C. Feelings (rate 0–10)	D. Evaluate and challenge unhelpful thoughts	E. New feelings (rate 0–10)
			Thinking errors *Evidence* *Alternatives* *Action*	

Thought Record

A. Situation	B. Thoughts (rate 0–10)	C. Feelings (rate 0–10)	D. Evaluate and challenge unhelpful thoughts	E. New feelings (rate 0–10)
			Thinking errors	
			Evidence	
			Alternatives	
			Action	

Thought Record

A. Situation	B. Thoughts (rate 0–10)	C. Feelings (rate 0–10)	D. Evaluate and challenge unhelpful thoughts	E. New feelings (rate 0–10)
			Thinking errors *Evidence* *Alternatives* *Action*	